FOCUS ON TEENAGERS

Research into Practice

London: HMSO

ISBN 0 11 321975 X

CONTENTS

Acknowledgements

This report was prepared with the help of an advisory group. In addition, drafts were read by the three research teams whose work was reviewed, by other academics interested in this field, and by policy makers and practitioners. Furthermore, a one day seminar allowed a range of relevant professionals, carers, and young people to make a most valued contribution. Represented at the seminar were: young people 'looked after', the Who Cares? Trust, Centrepoint, The Trust for the Study of Adolescence, local authority children's homes, residential schools, secondary schools, local authority children's services, foster care, directors of social services, community paediatricians, and the Department of Health Social Care Group. I am grateful to all these and other colleagues who found time in their busy work schedules to supply accurate information, offer sound advice and meticulously correct drafts. In particular I would like to express my thanks to the Department of Health for its essential support.

Hedy Cleaver
University of Leicester

Preface

This publication draws out the messages for policy and practice from three recently published research studies, commissioned by the Department of Health, about teenagers in need. It is the fourth such volume since 1985 in which concise, practical lessons are distilled from research findings.

Over the past decade or more, the plight of the younger child in need of protection has absorbed much of the attention of public agencies, so that concern for teenagers in need has lost some emphasis and clarity. The research studies, upon which the overview is based, are therefore most timely. We are grateful to Hedy Cleaver of Leicester University for compiling the commentary and for extracting the key messages, to the three research teams for allowing their original studies to contribute to this project and to those who participated in a consultative capacity.

We hope *Focus on Teenagers* will be widely read by policy makers and practitioners in many agencies who will be encouraged to study in more detail the original research findings, and thereby fuel a resurgence of interest in teenagers in need.

Introduction

This publication focuses on teenagers and follows the tradition of the Department of Health to summarise and disseminate the findings of the child care research they have funded. Like its predecessors it aims to make key messages from the research accessible to social workers and demonstrate their relevance for policy and practice.

Previous exercises in research dissemination, 'Social Work Decisions in Child Care' (1985), 'Patterns and Outcomes in Child Placement' (1991) and 'Child Protection: Messages from Research' (1995) were based on a large range of different inter-related studies. This review explores the findings from three recently published Department of Health studies on teenagers and is therefore less ambitious. Because the research focused on a broad group of teenagers in need of social work services, those with specific problems such as physical disability or learning difficulties are small in number and their experiences should not be assumed to be widely representative. Nonetheless, the current research studies have important messages because, except for work on 'leaving care', they are the first to look specifically at the deployment of local authority services in relation to teenagers and the outcome of these efforts.

Unlike the Department of Health's research initiative into Child Protection, the research focusing on teenagers was not commissioned as a package. Although one could argue that opportunities for cross fertilisation were missed, it does make the identification of similar themes particularly striking. For example, each study highlighted the importance of family and wider kin, of professionals engaging in direct work with young people and of recorded plans and packages of care.

The Children Act 1989 established the principle of shared parental responsibility. The following overview adopts the position that the state, where possible in co-operation with the family, has an obligation to ensure that teenagers in need of social work services are given the best possible start to adult life. To explore how successful local authorities are at fulfilling this duty, the findings from the research are explored by comparing young people's experiences with a best scenario position. By this we mean what we would ideally want for teenagers on a number of recognised criteria important to young people's quality of life (Parker et al., 1991; Bullock et al., 1994).

The structure of the book resembles earlier dissemination exercises. Contained in the **introduction** is a quick guide to the three research studies and a brief exploration of how recent legal and administrative changes may affect vulnerable teenagers. The **overview** identifies the principal messages arising from the three studies, examines common themes, produces observations and findings not immediately apparent from reading the individual reports, and discusses the implications for policy and practice. The third section consists of short **summaries** written by the authors of the three research projects. The final part refers the reader to a range of relevant existing **tools, check lists and exercises** and gives a brief description of each.

A guide to the three research studies

The Department of Health is concerned about a range of aspects concerning children and young people and has funded a substantial body of research to inform practice and guide policy. The three research studies, funded by the Department of Health, and reviewed here, focus on social work services for teenagers and include:

Social Work and Assessment with Adolescents,
Ruth Sinclair, Louise Garnett and David Berridge,
National Children's Bureau, 1995.
Research director – Ruth Sinclair.

Teenagers and the Social Work Services,
John Triseliotis, Moira Borland, Malcolm Hill and Lydia Lambert,
HMSO, 1995.
Research director – John Triseliotis.

Moving On: Young People and Leaving Care Schemes,
Nina Biehal, Jasmine Clayden, Mike Stein and Jim Wade,
HMSO, 1995.
Research director – Mike Stein.

The authors' summaries can be found later in this publication but in order to appreciate the strengths and weaknesses of the ensuing discussion, it is important to have some understanding of the key areas covered by the individual studies. The following table offers the reader a comprehensive guide to the three research studies.

A comparison of the three research study designs

	Assessment Research: Sinclair et al.	Teenage Services Research: Triseliotis et al.	Leaving Care Research: Biehal et al.
Criteria for inclusion in study	Assessment because: a. considered for care b. admission for care c. placement breakdown	Receiving social work services: a. 'looked after' b. supervised at home c. living independently	Leaving care: a. left care b. about to leave care
Age of teenager	10–16	13–18	16–19
Number studied	75	116	183 surveyed 74 studied
Follow-up time	12 months	12 months	18–24 months
Number of local authorities involved	1	5	3
Type of research	Qualitative and quantitative	Qualitative and quantitative	Large survey with qualitative sample
Method of investigation	Scrutiny of case records and interviews with social workers. A small number of interviews with teenagers, families and carers.	Primarily interviews with social workers, young people and birth families. Standardised tests used with teenagers.	Questionnaires for social workers. Interviews with young people, social workers and scheme workers for the qualitative study.

Common Threads

The table illustrates how the three studies could be seen as sequential in that each focused on a different stage in the story of 'social work services for teenagers'. The assessment research looked at assessment and included in their sample teenagers not yet in the system – those 'considered for care', the teenage services research focused on young people within the system and examined the effects of social work services, while the leaving care study explored the experiences of young people making the transition into the adult, 'independent' world. Thus, each has a unique contribution to make to the overall picture.

The sample groups involved in the three research projects were, however, not discrete. For example, there was considerable overlap in the age structure of the three samples and some convergence of the selection criteria used by the different studies. In the assessment research sample practically two thirds of assessments involved teenagers who were either admitted to care or already within the system; criteria which would have made them eligible for inclusion in the study of teenage services. Similarly 17% of this sample group moved into independent living during the study period and thus were synonymous with the sample used in the leaving care research. As a result, although each study provides a valuable and distinctive contribution, the over-lapping criteria of the sample groups substantially strengthen the general research messages.

Overview

1. Teenagers: Areas of change and role transition

The teenage years are a period distinguished by change and transition (Coleman and Hendry, 1990). The onset of puberty in early adolescence is heralded by behavioural changes, sudden growth and major restructuring of physique. Alongside the physical changes, a similar revolution takes place in cognitive ability, social relationships, and social and psychological autonomy.

Late adolescence is also marked by important role transitions. It is a time when many young people leave school, learn to drive, vote, fall in love, start work, or set up a home of their own.

It is also an age when the frequency of many psycho-social disorders increases. But it would be misleading to assume that the majority of teenagers are affected. Research shows this applies to no more than 15% of young people in the general population (Rutter, 1990). However, teenagers in need of social work services are particularly vulnerable, in that they present a range of acute and chronic problems which single them out from the majority of their peers. Packman and Hall's (1995) research shows that behaviour was a matter for complaint in practically all teenagers who were accommodated. *'Eight out of ten (80%) of the young people were described as excessively argumentative and chronic rule-breakers; seven out of ten (71%) were runaways; six out of ten (61%) truanted from school; and forty five per cent were described as aggressive, and sometimes violent'* (Packman and Hall, 1995: 99). The degree and persistence of their problems made them more prone to difficulties when making role transitions, than the majority of young adults. Indeed, as the following sections will show, when teenagers in need of social work services strive for self-sufficiency and independence many become homeless, and when they seek a job the majority end up unemployed.

This overview examines the three research studies and other relevant research to explore how well social service intervention prepares young people for the transitions facing them and compares this with what we would ideally want for teenagers. To do this, dimensions based on work by Bullock and colleagues (1994) and the criteria developed to assess the progress of individual children 'looked after' (Parker et al., 1991; Ward, 1995) have been used. The concepts arising from these two publications are complementary because Bullock and colleagues' ideas informed the Independent Working Party established by the Department of Health to develop the criteria for 'Assessing Outcomes in Child Care' (Parker et al., 1991). Although the criteria were developed to examine outcomes of individual children, they provide a useful framework to explore important role transitions and assess the impact of social service provision.

The framework focuses on six areas of teenagers' lives: **Health and health education; Education, training and employment; Behaviour and emotional development; Relationships; Identity; and Life skills.** Under each heading the research findings are explored in terms of teenagers' problems, the success or otherwise of local authorities to assess current needs and adequately address deficits, and outcome for the young person vis-a-vis their ability to cope with adult living.

a) Health and health education

The physical upheaval which takes place during adolescence can confuse and distress some teenagers. For example, many girls dislike the changes puberty wreaks on their bodies and fuelled by media pressure strive to retain or regain their childlike figures '. . . *by late teens and early twenties, up to half of girls have dieted, usually without success'* (Leffert and Petersen, 1995: 69).

Adolescence also brings an increase in male sex hormones which stimulates the sex drive in both genders. As a result it is a time when many young people embark on their first sexual encounter. But unless teenagers have received adequate preparation, sexual experimentation can endanger their health, either through the contraction of sexually transmitted diseases or the complications of early, unwanted pregnancy. This risk increases for teenagers in need of social work services – research has shown that sexual relationships are more likely to take place sooner rather than later for more vulnerable teenagers (Leffert and Petersen, 1995).

Other types of experimentation may also affect the health of teenagers – smoking, drug, alcohol or substance abuse can all have negative consequences.

When children grow up within the bosom of their birth family, most parents accept that physical care and health education, are basic parental tasks. But when young people are 'looked after' by a local authority the successful assumption of this responsibility can be hampered by a number of factors. For example, no one person may have a comprehensive knowledge of the teenager's medical history, or over-all responsibility for their health and there may be confusion over who should actively promote the teenager's health and health education (Parker et al., 1991).

There are few research studies which focus on the health of children 'looked after' and what does exist suggests this may be an area which requires greater attention. For example, an analysis of data from the National Child Development Study by Lambert (1983) found children in care to have many health problems. More recently, Packman and Hall's (1995) study of accommodated children shows 1 in 10 suffered from varying forms of ill health and twice as many had non acute medical needs – such as hearing loss, poor sight or impaired mobility.

Issues of teenagers' general health or their need for health education were not often high on the list of social workers' priorities when working with teenagers. The assessment research illustrates this lack of attention at the assessment stage. Although the policy statement of the participating local authority sought a '. . . *detailed and thorough multi-disciplinary assessment of the physical, emotional, social and educational needs of children and young people whose needs were not being met or who were at risk of losing their families . . .'* few social workers had seen the document so most were unaware of the principles and how they might be operationalised when assessing young people (Sinclair et al., 1995: 131).

Although general health was not commonly an aspect of assessment, specific problems such as extreme conduct disorder or bizarre behaviour did trigger the involvement of health specialists. Unfortunately, their participation did not automatically result in more informed decision making. A number of factors including social workers' access to specialists, the different time-scales particular professions work to, and a failure to gain the co-operation of young people and their families, were shown to impede a timely completion of specialist assessments.

Securing the agreement of young people was also found to be key in the implementation of statutory medical examinations. Less than a quarter of teenagers admitted to care had undergone a statutory medical examination and for many this was because young people had with-held permission (Sinclair et al., 1995). Such a poor response suggests that the current statutory medical examination was not perceived by either teenagers, families or social workers as relevant. These findings raise the question of whether the present practice, with its emphasis on physical examination, should be reconsidered.

When teenagers were 'looked after' or supervised at home social work records noted details of chronic or serious physical illness and psychiatric disorders. Indeed records showed that at least 40% of young people receiving social work services had at some point been referred to a psychologist or psychiatrist. However, reference to more mundane aspects of health care, such as weight, teeth, ears or eyes was less likely (Triseliotis et al., 1995).

The teenage services study used the perceptions of young people, parents and social workers to gain a measure of young people's health. From this we learn that the majority of teenagers receiving social work services considered their general health to be good during the study year. Girls appeared to be more prone than boys to ill health, both by their own and their social workers' account. Almost half the young people said they had had some '. . . *particular health problems*' during the year (Triseliotis et al., 1995: 222). The health issues most frequently mentioned by both boys and girls were those likely to afflict young people generally and included broken bones or injuries (often sports related), infections of various kinds, and eating problems.

In addition to injuries and illnesses 71% of adolescents receiving social work services admitted to smoking, 65% to drinking, over a third to taking illicit drugs and 13% to abusing solvents, occasionally or frequently. Comparisons with national figures are difficult because the methods used to collect and categorise this type of data vary. Nonetheless they suggest that, except for alcohol consumption which appears similar, teenagers in need of social work services are more than twice as likely to smoke, take illegal drugs or abuse solvents than young people of similar age in the general population (Balding, 1995; Baker and Marsden, 1994; OPCS, 1995). This behaviour took place despite the fact that nearly all the young people said they were aware of the dangers of these activities and the majority (86%) had received advice and information (Triseliotis et al., 1995).

Social workers took teenagers' smoking, drug and alcohol misuse seriously and this was found to dominate many of their discussions with young people. Attempts to influence smoking or alcohol/drug use are notoriously difficult because, while the gratification is instant, the negative effects on health are delayed and uncertain. Success was shown to depend on young people making a personal commitment to change their habits. Attempts by professionals to encourage them in this direction by acting as a mentor were effective only if done within a relationship of trust. Trust between social workers or carers and young people takes time to develop and for many teenagers 'looked after', continuity of relationships was in short supply. Nonetheless, in half of cases where social workers tried to change young people's habits the intervention was considered to have been successful (Triseliotis et al., 1995). But the difficulties facing social workers who attempted to bring about positive change, were reflected in the leaving care research which found some 17.5% of their initial sample of 74 reported they had a drug problem or were perceived by professionals to have a problem with drug use (Biehal et al., 1995: 273).

Issues around sex were often neglected when teenagers were living away from home. One in four teenagers, in the teenage services research, claimed not to have been informed about the risks of unsafe sex and social workers felt that most young people needed help to prepare for close personal relationships. Several factors may account for this level of ignorance. For example, discussing such personal matters evoked acute embarrassment in one or other of the parties (Triseliotis et al., 1995). In addition frequent placement changes and school absenteeism resulted in some young people missing lessons covering sex education. A possible solution would be to give all teenagers 'looked after' health education pamphlets but, unless the young person has sufficient reading and cognitive skills, such an exercise would be pointless. Success in tackling sexual issues was found to depend on the quality of the relationship between the teenager and carer or social worker, and the willingness of professionals to broach the matter. Sadly, the leaving care study found that within 18-24 months of leaving care a third of young people had become parents. The study's finding that over half of pregnancies were unplanned suggests social workers' anxieties that counselling young people about sexual matters was frequently scanted, appeared to be well founded.

The task for social workers is complicated because however well they may explain the mechanisms of preventing pregnancy or AIDS this is frequently not enough. Research into the control of AIDS infection emphasised the tripartite need for young people to know the best preventive action, to develop the necessary coping strategies to act effectively, and to acquire sufficient self confidence to influence what happens to them (Bandura, 1990). To practice safe sex depends on communication between partners. The leaving care research suggests psychological factors are as important as practical information, '. . . *where young women have had poor chances for developing trust, confidence and a positive self identity, relating to young men in a confident and assertive way can be difficult'* (Biehal et al., 1995: 132).

To improve the general health of young people, social work services need to address issues of health and health education in assessment, planning and reviews. Health education requires more than supplying information. Young people whose behaviour undermines their health may experience difficulties in altering established habits and need the unstinting and continued support of someone they trust. The authoritative relationship between teenager and social worker can impede confidences and it may be judicial to co-opt other, specifically trained agency staff to discuss sensitive issues. When a position of trust has been established but events necessitate a change of key worker, serious consideration needs to be given to finding a way to continue the relationship, or to give the young person some choice in who will assume this role.

With the reforms in health provision, local authority social services departments will need to negotiate with Health Authorities and Trusts the services to be purchased for children and young people in their care. This reorganisation offers local authorities an opportunity to change radically the style and content of the health information they supply, and the medical checks and assessments on offer.

For young people and parents to attend medical assessments the service must be seen to be relevant to their needs.

b) Education, training and employment

Along with concerns over children's health, most parents also worry about education. Early schooling raises fewer anxieties but secondary school is perceived as the gateway to exciting careers and good jobs. Parents recognise what research has taken years to prove, that qualifications earned at the age of 16 are the best single predictor of the direction an individual's career will take (Banks et al., 1992).

Many adolescents who came to the attention of social services had a poor school career in comparison with their peers. Indeed more than two thirds of teenagers involved in the assessment research displayed problems with schooling and more than a quarter were out of school for over a year. These teenagers had come to dislike school, many had fallen behind in their education, some disrupted classes or were frequently absent (Sinclair et al., 1995). The legacy of educational problems was reflected in research into services for teenagers which found only half of school aged children 'looked after' or supervised at home were enrolled in mainstream schools. A further quarter attended residential or special schools or secure units, either temporarily or permanently. Teenagers excluded during their final year of compulsory education were particularly vulnerable because few alternative provisions were available (Triseliotis et al., 1995).

When teenagers were assessed, it was the negative aspects of their educational career – disruptive behaviour, learning difficulties and truancy – which understandably dominated professional perceptions. Indeed a policy of getting children back into school in order to improve their life chances has a firm theoretical base (Farrington, 1980; Hibbet et al., 1990). But in conjunction with tackling control issues social workers need to perceive education, with regard to the children they serve, as an enriching experience and place an equal emphasis on encouraging scholastic achievements (Jackson, 1989; Aldgate et al., 1993).

The prominence of school related problems among teenagers referred for assessment was not reflected in the attention given to education during the assessment process. The assessment research found less than a quarter of assessments, where teenagers were of school age, included an educational dimension, and less than half were ready in time for the planning meeting. Incomplete assessments and a failure to prioritise education might account for the finding that in 27% of cases there were no plans made for the young person's education or employment (Sinclair et al., 1995). The broader aspects of education, such as music, art or sports were rarely a consideration.

When children are 'looked after' parental responsibility is shared between parents and the local authority. Fletcher-Campbell and Hall (1991: 164) suggest that the local authority has '. . . *a responsibility to act as the 'most effective' parent rather than the 'normal' parent.'* Previous research indicates that in terms of academic achievement, many fall short of this ideal and that being 'looked after' by a local authority carries a high risk of educational failure (Jackson, 1989; Fletcher-Campbell and Hall, 1991). The recent report 'The Education of Children Who Are 'looked after' by Local Authorities' reinforces this '. . . *the education standards achieved by the children were too low.'* In particular it found that secondary school children '. . . *seldom reached standards close to those expected . . .'* (Social Services Inspectorate (SSI) and Office for Standards in Education (OFSTED), 1995: 3 & 11).

The experience of being 'looked after' by a local authority can exacerbate rather than ameliorate school related problems. The findings from the three studies reiterate the messages from earlier work and highlight a number of relevant factors. First, coping with the unhappiness and stress of care interfered with the ability to learn. *'They said I never used to work, I . . . went into a decline if you like, just sat there doing nowt, staring into space'* (Biehal et al., 1995: 60). Second, schooling was disrupted because keeping young people learning was not always seen by social workers as a fundamental issue when deciding on a placement. However, when education was a priority this could result in varied and innovative provision – half of those of school age involved in the teenage services research received some form of specialist educational provision including:

● individual home tuition

● day specialist education (within or away from main stream schools)

● day units within residential schools

● residential schools run by local authorities

● independent residential schools.

Third, young people 'looked after' rarely had anyone who acted as their champion. A champion would be someone who would oversee their educational progress, encourage their efforts, inculcate a respect for learning, and negotiate with schools and other institutions for better provision. The lack of such a person has been shown to adversely affect the educational progress of vulnerable young people (SSI and OFSTED, 1995; Cleaver forthcoming). Fourth, the value system and informal culture of the placement influenced young people's attitude to education. In many children's homes the situation appeared to have changed little from that highlighted a decade ago by Millham and colleagues (1981); books and newspapers were a rare commodity and an anti-authoritarian attitude was common-place among many residents, a stance which appeared to be tacitly accepted by some staff *'. . . in the end they just used to let us stay in bed . . . and not bother going to school . . . I used to be able not to go. I don't know why'* (a young woman's account of her experience, Biehal et al., 1995: 62). Finally, the results from all three studies reinforce the findings from the SSI and OFSTED (1995: 147) report which showed that when young people were 'looked after', education suffered because *'. . . educational needs often fall between the bureaucracy of Social Services and Education'.*

A failure to attend school [and the SSI and OFSTED (1995) report found a quarter of 'looked after' young people aged 14–16 had a history of poor attendance or were excluded] places additional stress on carers (Berridge and Cleaver, 1987). A low tolerance of disruptive behaviour in schools may be the result of a failure to appreciate the young person's circumstances. To prevent hasty exclusions, clear procedures are needed to share information between different agencies and enable effective liaison between social workers and teachers.

An improvement in educational achievement or school related problems was found to be associated with placements in stable foster homes (Biehal et al., 1995) and residential schools or units with education on the premises (Triseliotis et al., 1995). In these situations young people became more committed to obtaining qualifications, which in turn contributed to parental satisfaction and the likelihood of staying on at school after the age of 16. Continuity of schooling was shown to be essential in order for young people to complete academic courses and retain their relationships with teachers and peers. Additional features associated with the greater success of residential schools, included the atmosphere and regime, standard of work, smaller classes, pastoral care and a special or key teacher who negotiated with other agencies and professionals on behalf of the young person (Triseliotis et al., 1995). Findings similar to those shown by Weiner and Weiner (1990); who attributed greater educational success to *'good schools, with smaller classes geared specifically towards their needs . . . these schools were sensitive to the learning problems of institutionalised children'* (Weiner and Weiner, 1990: 47).

Despite examples of good practice the leaving care research found that: *'Between one half and three quarters of care leavers complete schooling with no qualifications'* (Biehal et al., 1995: 67). Hardly surprising then is their finding that the majority of teenagers who ceased to be 'looked after' fought shy of further education, or that unemployment rates for care leavers aged 16-19 years stood at more than twice the national average – some 50% were unemployed. Unemployed care leavers were shown to benefit from the central role leaving care schemes played in administering finances and, to varying degrees, from the pressure they exerted on authorities to discharge their discretionary powers to offer financial assistance under Section 24 funding.

Many young people with whom leaving care schemes worked, had embarked on an insecure career path where unemployment was punctuated by episodes on training schemes or casual work. Schemes varied in their approach, some offered a drop-in facility where career advice was available and job vacancies could be checked, others ran regular sessions with a careers officer, but the majority of schemes gave help on a one to one basis. Unlike the partnerships and formal links that leaving care schemes had developed to secure suitable accommodation and finances, links with colleges, employers and training agencies to promote young people's education/work careers were in their infancy.

There were examples of good practice where assistance with education or employment formed part of a comprehensive package of support. But the overall finding cannot be escaped and makes depressing reading. *'The four schemes appeared to have little impact on educational progress and on employment patterns despite some work in these areas'* (Biehal et al., 1995: 275). Education, training and job opportunities are clearly areas where there remains a serious need for many local authorities to take a pro-active approach.

To support young people who are causing concern in school or to encourage those who have rejected school to return to education, calls for innovation at both an individual and general level. On a personal basis, teenagers require a champion who believes in their ability, finds out what type of provision they find acceptable, promotes their cause, and negotiates with the relevant agencies to secure the most appropriate educational facility. In addition, the education of all young people 'looked after' would benefit from the type of joint Social Services and Education Authority approach recommended by the Department for Education guidelines (DfE and DoH, 1994b).

Although this style of initiative is widely accepted as the way forward (SSI and OFSTED, 1995), it can be hampered by different professional philosophies. For example, teachers want an early warning system which allows problems to be identified promptly so speedy intervention can prevent difficulties escalating, while social workers fear labelling youngsters and seek intervention often as a last resort. The ability of the local education authority to influence what goes on in schools has been diminished by the introduction of local management (see the Education Act, 1988). One consequence is that social services will need to establish separate arrangements regarding teenagers 'looked after' with individual schools. Needless to say, unless an effective working partnership is developed between local education departments and social services departments and schools, misunderstandings over different aims, objectives and priorities will continue, joint preventative work will remain a rarity and any alternative provision will stay out of reach for 1 in 5 excluded teenagers (SSI and OFSTED, 1995).

c) Behaviour and emotional development

'It is important to include behavioural and emotional development as a dimension for assessment since many children are 'looked after' by local authorities because they have difficulties in these areas which their families and schools are unable to contain . . . when attention to these issues reveals problems they ought not to be regarded as inevitable concomitants of 'care' but rather as conditions which may be amenable to skilled treatment' (Parker et al., 1991: 93).

Young people's behaviour and emotional development are difficult to look at in isolation because they affect all aspects of their lives. For example, challenging and aggressive behaviour in school may lead to exclusion with all its concomitant problems or alternatively a fear of failure or boredom can cause teenagers to misbehave. Similarly drug or alcohol misuse may be the result of deep seated emotional problems and drunken or 'high' teenagers can behave in frightening ways.

Over three quarters of young people referred for assessment were thought by professionals to be displaying disturbed or disturbing behaviour (Sinclair et al., 1995). A figure consistent with the teenage services research which found the behaviour of 80% of young people was rated as above the cut-off point for disordered behaviour (data was derived from asking teenagers, parents and social workers to complete an adaptation of the Rutter scale, (Rutter et al., 1970). This incidence of disturbance may yet be an underestimation because disturbed behaviour which does not challenge adult rules is frequently unrecognised. For example, the majority of 14 year olds in Rutter and colleagues (1976: 41) general population study reported '. . . *some appreciable misery or depression . . .*' but in the majority of cases this had failed to be identified by either parents or professionals. The silent and withdrawn adolescent can easily be overlooked by teachers battling with hectic classes or by carers trying to cope with a range of pressing concerns.

The emotional and behavioural problems displayed by teenagers in need of social work services have long antecedents. At the assessment stage a fifth of young people had, at some point in their past, been on the local authority Child Protection Register and a similar proportion had previously been in care or were known to the Department as a result of offending (Sinclair et al., 1995). Because the problems were long standing, many families had become polarised. Parents felt embattled, hopeless, useless and tired, while others admitted to feelings of despondency and helplessness.

Difficulties escalated as age gave teenagers greater independence and parental threats were countered by defiance and/or departure. This shift in the balance of power left some parents feeling incapable of controlling their teenager and led to reports of feeling *'shattered and depressed', 'being at breakdown point', 'feeling drained and a failure'* (Triseliotis et al., 1995: 66). However, some social workers, through skilful and delicate negotiations, were able to obtain a better balance between parental or carers' expectations and the wishes of young people.

Mothers took the brunt of the young person's disordered behaviour and a few became frightened by the aggression and violence of their teenage children. The account of one mother illustrated this mixture of helplessness and despair. *'I just told them I'd had enough. I couldn't cope. I'd tried everything. She was well into drugs and God knows what else . . . I wanted her to be safe. Not happy but safe. So I told them, 'she's your responsibility now'. I didn't know what else I could do'* (Sinclair et al., 1995: 103). As difficulties escalated parents came to see themselves as victims of their children. One consequence of this was that problems were not conceived of in a dynamic way and parents placed all the responsibility and onus for change on the young person.

At the assessment stage, increased resources were focused on teenagers with the greatest problems. Severe behavioural or emotional problems triggered specialist assessments. Psychiatric or psychological assessments were sought for suicidal or self-mutilating teenagers, health professionals mobilised for severe drug/alcohol misuse, and specialist residential resources for teenagers with anti-social and aggressive behaviour (Sinclair et al., 1995). The problems surrounding the use of specialist assessments, noted in the section on young people's health, resulted in less than a quarter of psychiatric and family therapy assessments being ready for the decision and planning meeting (Sinclair et al., 1995). To use the best possible services for the most disturbed teenagers, though laudable, is of questionable value if decisions are made without the benefit of their findings. Perhaps as a result plans with regard to teenagers' behaviour were restricted to broad objectives rather than making specific reference to addressing their behavioural needs (Sinclair et al., 1995).

Some types of social work intervention were more successful than others in bringing about a change in young people's behaviour. When teenagers were supervised at home, although much of social workers' time was spent talking to young people and their parents about problematic behaviour, neither parents nor teenagers felt it had been particularly effective (Triseliotis et al., 1995). A possible explanation for this singular failure is offered by previous studies, which suggest positive outcomes are related to shared perspectives (Fisher et al., 1986; Cleaver and Freeman, 1995). In fact, the teenage services research found no such congruence over how best to resolve problem behaviour – social workers saw the intervention as an opportunity to work on developmental needs, families wanted their teenagers controlled, while the young people looked for practical solutions. But respect for one position need not be at the expense of another and the expectations of all parties may have validity.

When adolescents are placed away from home they present greater problems of control than younger children because they have the capacity to vote with their feet when things are not to their liking. Although most families exert control over teenagers either through fear or love, when young people are first 'looked after' or when placements change neither fear nor bonds of affection exist.

As already noted to develop a trusting and affectionate relationship with disruptive and/or disturbed adolescents takes time, but it also requires much patience and skill on the part of the professional. Unfortunately, the majority of staff employed in residential work with children and young people have been shown to lack a relevant qualification (SSI, 1991). A consequence of little training is that carers may feel helpless and threatened by bizarre, seemingly uncontrolled or violent behaviour. When this occurs one method of control is the administration of drugs, but a more common response in this country is to transfer the difficult adolescent elsewhere (Millham et al., 1978; Harris and Timms, 1993). This solution may solve the problems confronting carers, but is likely to increase young people's sense of rejection and failure and perpetuate the pattern of disrupted relationships.

A scrutiny of the different types of residential placements found schools to be more prepared than other residential institutions to hold on to their disruptive pupils. This allowed trust to develop, enhancing the chances for staff to influence young people's behaviour. The majority of parents of these teenagers thought the residential school had met or exceeded their expectations in terms of controlling the young person's behaviour (Triseliotis et al., 1995).

In contrast, foster placements showed more variability. In some cases young people greatly valued the experience and believed it had helped them to mature, control their more violent outbursts and keep out of trouble. But when no emotional bonds were formed, teenagers found foster carers unhelpful and restrictive, resenting what they interpreted as unwarranted nagging.

A substantial proportion, but not all, of those showing delinquent activities or conduct disturbances in childhood and adolescence go on to exhibit pervasive and persistent social malfunction in adult life (Robins, 1978/1986; Farrington, 1991; Zoccolillo et al., 1992). But the likelihood of problem behaviour carrying on into adult life is influenced by factors operating in childhood, such as poor peer relationships, attentional problems and hyperactivity (Farrington et al., 1990; Magnusson and Bergman, 1990). Somewhat reassuring then, is the finding that social work intervention and service provision was considered by parents, teenagers and social workers to have stopped or reduced behaviour problems in half the cases (Triseliotis et al., 1995). Children's powers of recovery are considerable and the present studies suggest that it is never too late to intervene. *'There is no excuse for giving up on the grounds that the child is too old for anything to make any difference'* (Rutter, 1985: 395). Nonetheless, despite these signs of improvement, there is little cause for complacency because the majority of teenagers in the teenage services research continued to show levels of disturbance above those normally seen in the general population.

The present system generally assumes single service provision – a placement in a foster home, a residential setting, or supervision at home with services such as befriending or group work. A young person's needs however, may be multiple, or change rapidly as they mature or circumstances alter. A more eclectic approach, involving a number of 'known' placements and a range of services, would ensure teenagers' needs are more readily met. To set this in place social workers may have to cross departmental boundaries and/or work in close liaison with other agencies, because the research has shown that one of the most important elements of successful service packages was the involvement of a combination of complementary inputs (Triseliotis et al., 1995).

d) Relationships

Adolescence is a stage when young people start to gain a degree of autonomy and independence from their family; while the influence of parents is reduced, peers become increasingly important. But regardless of this shift, except for a minority of youngsters, peer influences rarely replace that of parents (Rutter et al., 1976). Thus, the family of origin remains important to most young adults throughout their transition from dependence to independence.

For young people in need of social work services, family relationships have often been volatile and unstable for some considerable time and a breakdown in the parent/teenager relationship was a common cause for young people to be referred for assessment. Reconstituted families were particularly susceptible to problems as teenagers perceived new partners or step-parents as monopolising their birth parent or unjustly curbing their behaviour (Sinclair et al., 1995).

The parent/child relationship, however, is complex and multi-layered. On the surface it may be turbulent and hostile and the damage apparently irreparable, but delve deep and a bedrock of loyalty and commitment is revealed. Mothers were found to bare the brunt of teenagers' recalcitrant and rebellious behaviour but nonetheless remained the first person to whom many turned to for support (Triseliotis et al., 1995). Families with teenagers need help to resolve conflicts.

The studies show that, unlike social work with families of young children, when teenagers were involved, provision of services under Part III of the Children Act 1989 was less likely. Many of the cases involving teenagers in crisis were known to social services, but professional support was rare and previous requests for assistance from parents frequently failed to result in any practical help (Sinclair et al., 1995). As a result when social workers did intervene and offer services, many parents were exhausted and disillusioned, and saw accommodation as the only remaining option.

In some families relationships improved with time. The teenage services research found half the parents and young people 'looked after' or supervised at home believed things had taken a turn for the better, either in terms of the amount of contact or the quality of the relationship. Relationships with siblings and other relatives, however, were relatively static and poor relationships with step parents were particularly persistent (Triseliotis et al., 1995).

But improvements were not always attributed to social services' intervention. For example, although the majority of parents credited social workers for making things better, teenagers were less likely to do so. Indeed, as often as not when relationships did improve this was considered to be '. . . *despite rather than because of the social worker'* (Sinclair et al., 1995: 209). One of the problems appears to be that, although there was much consistency among social workers on the need to improve family relationships, there was less over how this could best be accomplished. Social workers who deployed mediation skills and worked towards resolving conflicts were more effective, and even some very shattered relationships were improved by this style of intervention.

In cases where relationships with parents had become irreconcilable, relatives were seen by some teenagers as sources of support. Sadly, poor relationships between teenager and parent were often accompanied by a lack of wider family support and practically half of referred teenagers were considered by their social workers to have no or very poor family networks (Sinclair et al., 1995). For young people devoid of adult support the outlook was bleak, particularly as social workers were sometimes unaware of their isolation.

When young people are placed away from home it is generally accepted that for the majority, contact with their birth families should be encouraged. Unfortunately, not all recorded plans reflected this maxim. Contact was part of the assessment plan in less than half of the cases where young people were 'looked after' (Sinclair et al., 1995). The teenage services research suggests this discrepancy between theory and practice may be the result of previous failures at family work resulting in some social workers becoming disillusioned (Triseliotis et al., 1995).

Placements away from home also affected young people's wider social network. Practically half the teenagers 'looked after', in the teenage services research, lost contact with earlier friends, while three-quarters made new friends. To apply simple profit and loss accounting to young people's social network obscures the different degree of obligation and loyalty inherent in long established friendships compared to the shallow bonding that applies to newly formed alliances. Moreover, young people exposed to continual change were found to be wary of investing in new relationships and as a result became increasingly isolated (Biehal et al., 1995).

By the time young people ceased to be 'looked after', well over a quarter had little or no contact with their parents or extended family. For many, this pattern was established before they were separated from their parents. The continuing symbolic and practical role families play in the lives of most young people 'looked after' was reaffirmed at the point of transition to independent living. The impending move stimulated some to renegotiate contact with parents or relatives, although sadly this usually resulted in further rejection and distress. *'I expected me family to mean more, think more of me and try to support me more . . . You see, it's the people that aren't related that seem to care more for us which seems funny'* (a young person discussing an attempt to re-establish contact, Biehal et al., 1995: 87).

Young people who ceased to be 'looked after' at 16-18 rarely returned to live at home; and birth parents were able or willing to offer support in only a third of cases. But it would be a mistake to assume teenagers did not value their families. Most viewed their relationship with parents as important and the majority had some contact during the early months after leaving care. Young people saw parental offers of help as a sign that someone cared about them and cherished the feeling that there was a place they could call 'home', even if they did not actually live there. For some (a fifth of the sample) extended family and in particular siblings, provided this support (Biehal et al., 1995).

The importance of prioritising family work during assessment and planning, as well as while adolescents are 'looked after', was illustrated by the experiences of care leavers. A low level of contact between separated teenagers and their families was related to little or no support on leaving. This was exacerbated for many by their similar lack of supportive relatives or friends. To assume that substitute carers will take on this role was found to be unrealistic. Only a third of fostered teenagers remained in contact with or were supported by their carers after leaving and very few were able to live with them after reaching the age of 18 years. For most, fostering failed to provide a substitute family or a stable home base which could be relied upon in the longer term (Biehal et al., 1995).

Leaving care schemes were aware of the vulnerability, loneliness and poor social networks experienced by many of their clients. The leaving care research found that approximately one quarter of teenagers involved with schemes were socially very isolated and entirely dependant on scheme support. Schemes attempted to address the isolation of young care leavers, not so much by working on family relationships, but by trying to extend social networks. Success was variable and while some young adults felt they had improved their skills in forming or sustaining relationships, others found their confidence and competence deteriorated. In terms of family relationships the study showed that, similar to earlier attempts by social workers to improve filiation, any reconciliation was rarely due to the actions of professionals. The schemes helped some very vulnerable young people by offering the presence of a consistent and concerned adult and practical assistance and support. But for many young people the aspect of the various leaving care schemes they prized most highly was the belief that someone cared about them.

e) Identity

Although an individual's identity is made up of a combination of 'given' elements it is also influenced by an understanding and interpretation of past events, the impact of present incidents and expectations for the future. As children enter adolescence they frequently question the belief system with which they were brought up. Parents' or carers' values may be discarded, however temporarily, as the influences of outside experiences and friends make their mark. During the transition from child to adult, many young people, secure in the knowledge of their early history, experiment with a range of different identities – free-spirited youth, earnest student, or dependant child – depending on their immediate circumstances.

The importance of a clear sense of personal history is widely acknowledged and social workers have come to recognise that children and young people, who spend large parts of their lives separated from their families, need to know not only who they are and where they have come from, but to understand why they are being 'looked after'. For many young people the experience of being 'looked after' leaves them confused and ill informed about past events. In these situations even tenuous links with parents, siblings and other relatives proved valuable for young people's understanding of their background (Biehal et al., 1995).

The Children Act 1989 recognises the need to promote actively a sense of identity in children 'looked after' by enjoining Local Authorities to consider '. . . *the child's religious persuasion, racial origin and cultural and linguistic background'* [Section 22(5)(c) of the Children Act 1989] when making placement decisions. To match carer and child successfully along all these dimensions may not always be possible but present practice appears to uphold some aspects at the expense of others. Recent social work literature, and the current three studies are no exception, suggests race tends to dominate practitioner concerns when placing children away from home. Nevertheless, to disregard strongly held religious beliefs and practices, cultural background or language, which is against the requirements of the Children Act 1989, is likely to antagonise families, particularly those from minority religious persuasion and/or those whose religious beliefs or cultural identity are central to their lives. For some young people placed away from home, familiar religious customs and cultural practices can give a sense of belonging and offer support and reassurance (Seden, 1995).

Much social work practice around issues of race is based on the premise that a black identity is a necessary political response because irrespective of whether teenagers are black, Asian or of mixed heritage, society will treat them in similar discriminatory ways (Small, 1986). This has given rise to a consensus amongst many social workers that unless black and mixed parentage children are 'looked after' in same race placements they will fail to develop a positive self-image or the coping skills to counter the racism they will inevitably face. Work by Tizard and Phoenix (1993), however, suggests that such a simplistic view may not always serve the child's best interest. Their research found that the majority of mixed parentage young people held very positive feelings about their mixed heritage (Tizard and Phoenix, 1995). The present studies also found that some mixed parentage young people held subtle and complex perspectives of their ethnic identity (Biehal et al., 1995).

The assessment research showed that supportive social work with African and Asian Muslim communities was not common. This could account for the finding that some of these families were unaware of what services were available, others were unwilling to expose private family matters to public scrutiny, while some were fearful of official reactions. A combination of these factors may be germane to the reluctance of African and Asian parents to seek social services' help. Indeed, most referrals involving teenagers from these communities emanated from other agencies or young people themselves (Sinclair et al., 1995).

Problems in working with families of different religious, cultural or ethnic backgrounds were confounded when social workers had little experience of the communities or their belief systems. When this was the case cultural stereotypes and personal feelings of insecurity and ignorance hampered pro-active work. For example, working with Muslim families posed problems for social workers because many were unsure of how best to balance respect for traditional family culture with teenagers' wishes (Sinclair et al., 1995). When conflict exists social workers must assess the young person's level of maturity and work with them to try and ensure they understand the implications of rejecting the customs and religious practices of their childhood.

Just as a general sense of identity is linked to a feeling of belonging to one's family, the ethnic classification used by black and mixed parentage teenagers was closely bound up with their acceptance or rejection of their family (Sinclair et al., 1995). Although the local authority involved in assessment research was a London Borough with a diverse ethnic and cultural community, issues of race, culture, religion and language were not found to be prominent in the policy or practice guidelines governing assessments. In contrast, the majority of social workers employed by the borough did recognise the importance and complexity of issues around identity although many felt unsupported by their local authority (Sinclair et al., 1995).

Difficulties in sustaining a young person's sense of identity when separated from their families was also an issue which concerned many of the social workers involved in the research into teenage services. The research found 47% of social workers thought young people needed more information and/or greater understanding of their family history. In contrast only 19% of the teenagers said they felt ignorant about their past but when they did this was associated with low self-esteem. The authors suggest this disparity between the perceptions of young people and their social workers was because young people concentrated on gaps in their knowledge about specific people or events, while social workers stressed the need for a greater understanding of past events (Triseliotis et al., 1995).

Issues around identity rarely formed part of the social work plan and only a third of the young people who wanted more information about their family background at the outset of the intervention improved their understanding during the subsequent year. When teenagers did find out things about their past it was mainly as a result of talking to relatives or accessing their own files (Triseliotis et al., 1995). A sense of cultural, religious or ethnic identity was shown to be augmented for separated young people by integration into and/or links with relevant religious and ethnic neighbourhoods and communities, placements with carers who shared similar backgrounds, contact and identification with parents, and friendships with peers who had similar roots (Biehal et al., 1995).

The number of care leavers who were black or of mixed heritage included in the sample for the leaving care research, was small. Their finding that these groups appeared little different from their white counterparts, in their degree of self-esteem, knowledge about their background and general sense of purpose, must therefore be viewed with caution. Definitions of self are complex and, as already indicated, likely to be affected by many aspects of young people's lives. For example, young people with a mixed cultural or racial heritage may review their allegiances as they form new links with different communities, different groups of friends, or one or other birth parent.

The leaving care schemes attempted to address care leavers' low self-esteem by improving practical and social skills with the belief that success in one area will increase the likelihood of success in others. Conquering the problems of living independently did improve levels of self-confidence and enhance self-belief. Positive experiences, such as a degree of rapprochement with family, a job or place on a course, or the birth of a baby, allowed young adults no longer 'looked after' to assume a new identity and see themselves in a more positive light. Unfortunately, just as success enhances self-respect and self-esteem, so failure undermines it. The most vulnerable teenagers were those with unresolved feelings about their past and a sense of powerlessness or low self-esteem. These young people tended to founder with the stresses and responsibilities of living independently whatever the level of support they received from social workers and/or leaving care schemes. However the continuity and support offered by the schemes meant that it was usually possible to put the pieces back together (Biehal et al., 1995).

For the young people involved in the leaving care research, the transition to adult independent living was a time when many attempted to make sense of their past and trace missing parents to find continuity in their lives and a sense of belonging. Piecing together a coherent story of their lives and understanding how and why events happened helped to provide a more secure platform for their future.

f) Life skills

The practical and social skills we need to survive as adults are learnt gradually throughout our childhood. The teenage years herald a period of re-negotiation as budding adults take up the banner for freedom – freedom to make choices, such as what to wear, who to associate with or when to engage in sexual relations. On the other side, parents and carers wave the flag of responsibility, struggling to push recalcitrant teenagers towards maturity, sobriety, practical skills and 'appropriate' behaviour. As a result of these different priorities there may be perturbations in the relationship, but families usually reach some common understanding (Collins, 1990). For most young people the transition to adulthood takes place in a secure living situation where their needs and abilities dictate the pace. But regardless of how able the young person is, unlike their compatriots in local authority care or accommodation, few find themselves living unsupported and independent lives at the age of 16–18 years.

Much research has shown that for young people 'looked after', the process of acquiring life skills was hampered because the practical arrangements of group living mitigated against individual freedoms, such as the ability to participate in decisions or take risks (Page and Clark, 1977; SSI, 1985; Berridge, 1985). Preparation for adult life was seen as something separate which could be compressed into the latter months of a young person's care career. Unfortunately, studies of young people leaving care at the age of 16–18 years belie the veracity of this assumption and show that many approach adulthood ill-equipped to manage on their own (Stein, 1990).

The present research indicates much social work practice continues to be guided by this false premise. Life skills were not a major element in the assessment of teenagers. The assessment research found that although guidelines issued to assessment foster carers and key residential workers by the specialist assessment service did make reference to looking at teenagers' *'level of maturity/ immaturity'* this rarely featured in reports, subsequent decision making, plans or service provision. For example, when young people were supervised at home, social workers' concerns about the adequacy of their life skills was generally triggered only when departure became imminent. Moreover, plans to help young people prepare for independence made at this late stage were just as likely to fail as to succeed (Sinclair et al., 1995).

Particular types of placement were more successful in preparing teenagers for adult life than others. When the foster placement enabled young people to 'feel part of the family', participate in family decision making, assimilate practical skills and experiment with inter-personal relationships in a secure environment, they lived up to social workers' expectations. Unfortunately, foster placements involving teenagers were prone to breakdown and opportunities for personal development or the acquisition of basic skills were then interrupted or missed. There was little evidence that foster carers were given much guidance or assistance to develop a programme of preparation, or that teaching tangible life skills was part of any plan or review process (Triseliotis et al., 1995).

The restraints of communal living meant that residential placements were able to offer young people fewer opportunities to gradually acquire life skills than family homes. The shift system and staff changes reduced continuity of support and often bulk purchasing and catering arrangements hampered opportunities for young people to learn practical skills. Somewhat surprising, therefore, was the relative success shown by residential schools to provide a supportive environment, although as already mentioned, this owed much to their ability to hold on to troublesome pupils (Triseliotis et al., 1995). But regardless of the type of institutional care, preparation for adulthood was generally focused on the later stages of a young person's care career.

The degree to which teenagers were prepared for life in the community was related to their age and gender. Very young adults, and particularly young men, experienced difficulties in managing once they left care (Biehal et al., 1995). This suggests social workers and carers may need to review their expectations and practice when working with boys. Being 'looked after' for a longer period gave young people an advantage which was still evident two years later. Adequate preparation was the key to success because the majority of teenagers who left care equipped with the necessary practical and social skills continued to develop and refine them once living in the community (Biehal et al., 1995). Of concern was the proportion of young people who failed to cope; only a quarter of care leavers in the teenage services research believed they were coping one year after leaving care (Triseliotis et al., 1995).

Leaving care schemes approached the problem in different ways. Some offered young people the option of living in supported accommodation, allowing them further time to experiment and take risks in a sheltered environment. Unfortunately, for a few young people this was still not enough and after leaving they failed to sustain their newly acquired skills. However, not all care leavers wanted to live in supported accommodation and because this is a limited resource careful assessment is essential to ensure that the most vulnerable are targeted.

To have to live independently at age 16-18, irrespective of the level of life skills, was a daunting experience for most care leavers and when schemes and/or social workers offered reassurance, company and support this was much esteemed (Biehal et al., 1995). Young adults applauded schemes for their accessibility and informality, especially when drop-in centres and social activities allowed them to ask for help in an easy and undemeaning way. For adolescents who failed to cope or whose skills broke down under the pressures of poverty, rejection and loneliness, a safety net was required to prevent a descent into despair and/or homelessness. Plans made when young people are about to leave care need to anticipate the need for future short term intensive support and note possible resources including family members and past carers. Also identified in care plans should be a professional who will work on behalf of the young adult and bear overall responsibility for ensuring an open door policy to advice and support.

The concept of training for independence assumes that a concentrated effort at the end of a long career 'looked after' can compensate for years of disrupted personal relationships, a lifetime of buffeted self-confidence, missed opportunities to acquire practical skills and a chaotic approach to day to day living. Teaching life skills needs to be part of a through-care plan which begins with assessment, is built into plans and reassessed during reviews. Young people 'looked after' need a secure living situation where they are encouraged to assimilate psycho-social and practical skills, allowed to take risks and made to face the consequences of their actions.

2. Fundamental needs of teenagers

This exploration of what the three research studies reveal about young people's experiences in different areas of their lives has shown high levels of disadvantage and examples of good practice which benefited individuals. But the studies generally illustrate an unco-ordinated service which failed many, and a future we would not wish for teenagers. However, they also showed that regardless of the area focused on, be it teenagers' health, education or life skills, there were fundamental issues which affected young people's quality of life. In order for teenagers to make up lost ground and develop the skills necessary for adulthood, the unmistakable message arising from the research is their need for a **stable home base,** an adult to **champion** their cause, and someone whom they trust to advise them and act as **a mentor.** The following sections explore how able social work services were in providing these elements for the young people whom they looked after.

a) A stable home base

It is widely accepted that most children and young people thrive best when brought up by their families in a stable living situation which offers strong emotional ties. Unfortunately for many young people in need of social work services, instability and change were already common features in their lives. At the time of referral a quarter were from reconstituted families, practically half (46%) had had at least one previous experience of care, while others had moved between relatives and friends before the current crisis led to service provision (Triseliotis et al., 1995). Sadly, the spectre of unstable living arrangements followed this group throughout their teenage years; less than a quarter of teenagers 'looked after' remained at their original address a year after the causal event (Sinclair et al., 1995; Triseliotis et al., 1995).

It would be wrong to assume all movement has negative causes and effects. Research suggests that change in itself is not harmful but rather it is the feelings of rejection or unplanned upheavals which are damaging (Weiner and Weiner, 1990). But for many teenagers the circumstances in which they entered the system militated against careful assessment and planning. Consistent with earlier research (Millham et al., 1986; Packman et al., 1986) the current studies found, although most teenagers were known to social services, a high proportion of those accommodated were emergency admissions. As a result social workers were ill prepared and had little time for planning or consultation with teenagers and their parents. The possibility of ensuring a good match between the resources and abilities of carers and the needs of teenagers was also hampered by a scarcity of foster and residential placements – resources dictated the placement rather than the young person's wishes or needs. A similar situation was found to exist for many young people already in the system. Once again placement changes were unexpected and more than half of moves between placements and/ or home were unplanned (Triseliotis et al., 1995). Plans need to recognise and anticipate the possibility of change because adolescents, who display the degree of troublesome behaviour highlighted by the three studies, will be prone to placement disruption and breakdown.

The stability of young people's living circumstances was associated with the type of placement. Living at home provided adolescents with a better chance of stability than being 'looked after'. Even so, more than half of teenagers living at home spent the year after the precipitating incident shuttling between parents, relatives and friends as things 'got too hot to handle' in any one household (Sinclair et al., 1995).

Placements in residential institutions or with foster carers were vulnerable to disruption in that only a quarter lasted as planned. This rate of foster home break-down is similar to that found a decade ago (Berridge and Cleaver, 1987) and suggests that previous calls for more training and wider support have not always been heeded (Aldgate et al., 1989). Of interest is the finding that 60% of placements at residential school lasted as planned (Triseliotis, 1995). Their greater success could be partly accounted for by their lack of stigma and reputation for academic achievement (Millham et al., 1981). Much research has shown that effective institutions are those where young people, family and professionals believe tangible benefits are gained from the experience, be it physical care, more love and understanding, or academic achievements (Tutt, 1974; Millham et al., 1981; Kahan, 1980). But in addition to these factors, the research into teenage services suggests that flexible living arrangements were also an important element; half the young people who attended residential school also spent a substantial amount of time at home (Triseliotis et al., 1995).

Some form of placement stability is essential because the research has shown that a series of moves interrupted school careers, hampered a comprehensive scrutiny of health needs, interfered with the development of social and practical skills, disrupted friendships and links with family, and thwarted the ability to build relationships with carers. However, when young people are 'looked after' it may be unrealistic to expect a single placement to fulfil all their needs. Research into insitutional provision for children consistently shows a more complex approach can offer greater stability (Lambert, 1968; Weiner and Weiner, 1990; Triseliotis et al., 1995). Social work placement plans may need to incorporate a number of stable 'known' contexts, all or mainly based within the teenager's community, and include contingency arrangements. For example, the plan might include weekly boarding at state, private or special school, with weekends and holidays shared between foster carers and birth parents. It is essential, however, that plans have built-in flexibility which allows them to adjust quickly if and when a young person's circumstances change or crises arise.

Such a 'multiplex' placement plan would offer stability, allow resources to be pooled, and encourage responsibility for and knowledge about the young person to be shared. This would aid constancy in other areas of young people's lives and thus prevent the total upheaval which currently faces many young people when placements break down.

The responsibilities of adult living come early to young people 'looked after'. The majority of teenagers in England anticipated and were expected by professionals to leave their substitute homes before the age of 18 years, 16 in Scotland (Triseliotis et al., 1995). This pattern has changed little during the past decade (Stein and Carey, 1986). An expectation of departure did not guarantee that moves to independence were planned. A third of teenagers involved in the leaving care research, left care in an unplanned manner. But regardless of their style of departure, few young adults who had spent long periods 'looked after', returned to live at home or with relatives (Biehal et al., 1995). For these young men and women the most likely scenario was to live without the support of an adult, in private tenancy, hostel accommodation, a bedsitter or lodgings.

Life after local authority care or accommodation offered young people no greater stability of living circumstances than they had experienced within the system. Two months after leaving, a third of young men and women in the leaving care study sample, had moved two or more times and by two years this had been the experience of over half the group (Biehal et al., 1995). As previously noted, moving home does not necessarily have negative causes. Indeed, young adults may and do move house because they are able to afford better accommodation, as a result of personal relationships changing, or to take up jobs and educational places.

To an extent these reasons applied to young care leavers but for most the research tells a more depressing story. A significant proportion of care leavers lost or relinquished their tenancies for very negative reasons. Some found that after years in care, they could not cope with living alone, or failed to budget adequately and got into debt, some fell out with neighbours or suffered extremes of loneliness, others had their property over-run by other young people, an experience graphically described by one young adult, *'I think I just messed up . . . friends took over my life'* (Biehal et al., 1995: 214). Once tenancies were lost or initial living arrangements collapsed, teenagers frequently experienced a succession of short stays as they shuttled between friends, relatives and periods of homelessness. It is disquieting to note that in one study 22% of care leavers were homeless at some point during the initial two years after leaving care (Biehal et al., 1995).

Young people involved with leaving care schemes were often those who had experienced the most unstable early housing careers and it is encouraging to find that schemes were successful in helping this group find suitable accommodation. A key to their success was the establishment of joint planning and formal agreements with housing providers. These arrangements were shown to facilitate the development of a flexible range of services, thus providing young adults with some choice and an element of control over their lives (Biehal et al., 1995).

For the majority of teenagers 'looked after', change was endemic in their lives either because their behaviour led to families giving up on them or alternative placements breaking down. When faced with moves in accommodation many young people felt helpless and powerless. They believed few social workers took account of their wishes when deciding where they should live and likened the experience to being a parcel passed from one hand to another. For those wishing to take control of their lives the only apparent option was to adopt extreme measures, such as running away, attempting suicide or giving vent to anti-social outbursts. The present system provides parents and carers of young children with much support – health visitors, nursery placements and respite care, to name but a few. But all three studies indicated that preserving families or supporting placements was less prominent in social work intervention involving adolescents.

Plans need to take a more comprehensive perspective and anticipate change. The principle of shared care, not only between parents and carers but when expedient between more than one set of substitute carers, needs to drive social workers' thinking when planning the living arrangements for this vulnerable group. A 'multiplex' approach would allow for negotiated moves between a set of recognised carers and known situations. Potential carers must be identified during assessment and reviewed in subsequent planning meetings. At each stage it is essential that the wishes of the young person are explored and as far as possible incorporated into the plans, because dissatisfied teenagers have a tendency to vote with their feet. The 'multiplex' accommodation plan might incorporate both local authority resources and those of the immediate family, wider kin and friends.

Finally, the vulnerability of many young adults no longer 'looked after' means that continuing support is a necessity and for those most at risk, the opportunity of returning to a 'safe haven' for a short respite when circumstances overwhelm them. To set up such a provision would of course have resource implications but so does the present situation where moves are crisis-led and result in undue stress for all those involved.

b) A champion

In order to fulfil their potential and gain the most from the opportunities available, young people need someone who acts vigorously, persistently and painstakingly on their behalf – they need a champion. A champion would assume the responsibility for advocating for the teenager, fighting on their behalf, and ensuring plans are carried through and decisions implemented. For the majority of adolescents their family assumes this role. Any threat, whatever its cause, normally results in parents taking up the cudgels of war as the best medical advice is sought, an apparently vindictive teacher is confronted, or an irate neighbour soothed. Although the role diminishes as the child grows up, it rarely ends. Family members are frequently instrumental in helping young adults secure their first jobs, the benefits they are entitled to, suitable accommodation or a fair rent.

But in order to act as the young person's champion, a parent or family member must be in sympathy with the young person's plight, a situation not always apparent when families were in need of social work services. The assessment research found that conflict and tension at home was the central complaint in referrals arising from parents or teenagers. For these young people the wider family was not often able to act as a substitute, indeed, practically half of referred teenagers were considered by their social workers to have no or very poor family networks (Sinclair et al., 1995).

To ensure that someone takes on the duties of a champion, social workers need to assess initially the ability and willingness of parents and other family members to continue, or assume this role. The research suggests that at the start of service intervention, in many cases there is reason for optimism. The majority of parents felt positive about social workers and saw meetings as an opportunity to work in partnership with social workers on the problems posed by their teenage child. Unfortunately, over time this positive picture faded and parents frequently came to believe social workers were partisan and ignored or dismissed their wishes in favour of the teenagers' demands (Triseliotis et al., 1995).

Parents' attitude to professionals soured when social workers failed to keep their promises and were not available when needed, were too lenient over their teenage children's behaviour or education, excluded them in discussions, dismissed their point of view, or ignored them when they asked for help. In contrast, if social workers kept parents informed about developments, listened to what they had to say and allowed them to express emotions, parents felt supported even if there was little change in the young person's behaviour (Triseliotis et al., 1995). These are all aspects of successful partnership which have generally been incorporated into social work practice involving families with young children (Family Rights Group, 1991). The research findings suggest they are equally pertinent when working with parents of adolescents (Triseliotis et al., 1995).

Situations where teenagers are 'looked after' and family relationships have irretrievably broken down, raised the question of how able professionals are at assuming and sustaining the role of champion. To work on behalf of a particular teenager, social workers need to acquaint themselves with the young person's wishes and needs. At the assessment stage face to face contact between teenagers and their social workers was variable and less than a quarter of teenagers saw their social workers on a weekly basis.

Some social workers saw getting to know the young person as the responsibility of key workers or assessment foster carers. To delegate this duty to those who have day to day care is an obvious option but can result in unexpected problems. For example, although engaging with young people is an essential part of assessment, the focus is often on immediate needs and the carer's commitment is, by definition, time limited. The role of champion should be taken on by a professional who has a long term allegiance to the young person. Similarly, although substitute carers are expected to work on behalf of the young people in their care and ensure their needs are met, the high levels of placement turnover in both residential or foster homes can result in worrying numbers being cast adrift.

The evidence from the three studies showed that, without someone to champion their cause, many young people failed to reach their full potential. A champion also helped to ensure teenager's views were heard and attended to, particularly in intimidating situations such as group discussions, meetings or Hearings, and decisions taken were implemented (Triseliotis et al., 1995). Without someone to help put forward their case, teenagers frequently believed they failed to get their ideas and wishes across.

Leaving care schemes proved more successful in championing the cause of young care leavers in some areas of their lives than in others. In housing and finance, schemes demonstrated how the needs of young people could be promoted at both a general and/or an individual level. For example, the work of some schemes benefited all young care leavers in that they invested in and managed supported accommodation, facilitated access to good quality main stream housing, or ensured local authorities implemented their powers and provided care leavers with the available grants or income support. Their work with individual young men and women helped gain and support tenancies or access to funds. Equally illustrative of the way concerted championship can impact on the lives of young people was the leaving care research findings about areas where it was frequently missing. For example, leaving care schemes were in their infancy in promoting young people's education, training or employment and this was reflected in the poor career paths which most care leavers pursued (Biehal et al., 1995).

All three studies showed that at every stage in the process there was a need for an identified professional to work on behalf of the young person; whether to negotiate with a local school a route back into education, ensure health checks are carried out, negotiate for lower rents, or support applications for benefits. A champion ensures that things get done and the research suggests that for decisions to be implemented someone must fight tenaciously on behalf of young people. One of the conclusions from the assessment research resonates in the findings of all three studies and makes a strong case for social work plans to nominate a professional, acceptable to the young person, whose role it is to promote the adolescent's long term interests. *'Positive outcomes for young people depend less on the procedural framework per se, and more upon the quality of the social work intervention – the continuity of social work input; persistence and advocacy by the social worker on behalf of the young person;*

capacity to engage in direct work with the young person and their family; and the extent to which social services are dependent upon other agencies' (Sinclair et al., 1995: 282).

c) A mentor

The findings from the three studies show a stable living situation and some one to champion their cause, organise and tailor a package of services to meet the young person's needs, form the basic building blocks for work with adolescents. But it is also clear that this is rarely enough because many young people in need of social work services have poor or no relationships with their family and few friends. Their plight is heart rending; many are isolated, marginalised, lonely, depressed and have little self-esteem. More than anything else they want to know that somebody whom they trust, cares about them, is interested in what they do and will forgive them for minor transgressions. Unqualified love may not be a realistic expectation for anyone other than a parent, but ensuring that the young person has an adult who listens to what they say, is dependable and available, and prepared to support them no matter what they have done, should be a possibility.

In most families parenting incorporates both the role of champion (already discussed) and that of trusted mentor. But this is not always the case, indeed it is not uncommon for the various aspects of parenting to be assumed by different family members or a particular role to be delegated to an outsider, such as a long-standing family friend or school teacher. Similarly when teenagers are 'looked after', a single professional can take on all aspects of parenting, or they may be split between different carers, including members of the family, social workers, leaving care workers, or befrienders.

To have an adult to confide in and discuss emotions and problems with is particularly important during adolescence because this is a period full of opportunity and risk. Young people are faced with psychological and physical changes which thrust them into new behaviours at a time when society allows them greater freedom. Most teenagers are guided in their choices by their parents (Rutter et al., 1976) but when young people are in need of social work services they may have no-one to turn to for advice. In these situations it falls to the professionals to assume the role of mentor.

To develop a relationship of trust and work on behavioural and emotional problems, was once a major aim of much social work practice with teenagers. However, the current studies suggest that priorities in social services departments have shifted and now focus more on providing immediate material support at the expense of tackling fundamental needs. This scanting of direct work with young people concerned many social workers. *'What we have got good at is juggling demands, client brokering, we call it; and making decisions . . . the bit we have got bad at is the in-depth stuff. . . I feel there are not enough people who have experience of working at great depth with the young people and who are therefore able to ascertain with ease what are the young people's needs and to work with them'* (adolescent assessment service social worker involved in the assessment research, Sinclair et al., 1995: 283).

Trust and respect take time to establish and teenagers who had been 'looked after' for long periods were more likely to have formed trusting relationships with carers and/or social workers than more recent entrants. To build a relationship of trust with adolescents who have experienced a life-time of rejection and disappointment is no easy task. It was heartening to learn that social workers, who persevered in their attempts, were able to win the confidence of even the most disinterested and defensive of teenagers. The remark of one young person illustrates just how valuable this can be for some isolated teenagers. *'I really trust him – I think he's about the only person I really do trust'* (Triseliotis et al., 1995: 136).

Although trust was a major consideration in whether or not teenagers liked their social worker, 'getting on well', be it with foster carer, befriender, social worker or key worker, was not synonymous with trusting them. Although most teenagers found professionals easy to talk to, far fewer were willing to confide in them and discuss personal matters (Triseliotis et al., 1995). Teenagers made clear distinctions between enjoyable, friendly people and those they felt able to trust.

A mentor can play a strategic role in the lives of teenagers 'looked after' or supervised at home. The teenage services research found such a relationship was key to changing patterns of behaviour relating to sexuality, offending or drug misuse. But to tackle such sensitive and emotive aspects of adolescents' lives requires social workers to breach long established defences in order to establish mutual trust and respect. This proved particularly effective if social workers were tenacious, but non-threatening, when talking to teenagers and counselling them on the consequences of their behaviour. Teenagers valued professionals who didn't give up on them and appreciated interventions which helped them to restrain their behaviour. *'I could talk to her (SW) if I was in trouble or if I thought I was going to go pinching'* (Triseliotis et al., 1995: 155).

To assume the role of mentor and embark on a moral discourse without appearing critical requires much skill and a high level of self-confidence. Unfortunately, a common theme found in all three research studies was the low status, lack of support, scant supervision and training experienced by social workers and carers who work with adolescents.

The legacy of fractured family relationships and poor social skills resulted in many young adults who ceased to be 'looked after' continuing to need a trusted and respected professional for advice and support. In their eagerness to rid themselves of what is frequently seen as a stigmatising system and with the optimism of youth, some young people initially rejected professionals who offered help and continued support. But when things went wrong these same teenagers had few resources to call upon. *'At first I thought I don't need help and then I did but there was no one there to help me'* (Biehal et al., 1995: 214). In reality, less than one third felt able to rely on their family to help sort out practical problems.

Many teenage care leavers suffered from loneliness and the story of one young person poignantly pleads the case for social workers and carers to persevere in their offers of support. *'Some days I'm all right, I can sit and I enjoy it, but there's other times when I sometimes don't feel I can cope, when I sit and cry about it. That's the only way I can cope'* (Triseliotis et al., 1995: 196). The leaving care research found practically a quarter of all care leavers lacked any non-professional support. For the majority of young care leavers the most valued aspect of any professional intervention was knowing someone cared about them, was interested in them and would help when things became difficult.

'They're there when you need 'em' (Biehal et al., 1995: 185).

'I see her about once every fortnight. She came round the other day and we went out for a meal. If I need anything she's always there. I don't know what more she can do . . . She's never let me down' (Triseliotis et al., 1995: 197).

'If I'm stuck for anything I can come down and ask 'em questions and they'll help me out if they can . . . it's good to know there's somebody around to help you, definitely' (Biehal et al., 1995: 172).

Like adolescents and young people generally, those in local authority care and accommodation are faced with choices in practically all areas of their lives. But the studies have shown that many were handicapped by a past history of rule breaking and alienation. As a result, one of the greatest challenges facing professionals is to break through the barriers teenagers erect and gain their trust. Once this is achieved social workers have the opportunity to offer guidance and support, and an emotional sanctuary in which the young person may shelter.

The distinction teenagers made between liking professionals and being prepared to confide in them suggests there is a need for a range of staff to engage in direct work with adolescents. Because the dynamics of any relationship are complicated and cannot always be anticipated, care plans would benefit from ensuring a number of professionals work directly with the young person. This would have the added advantage of offering teenagers an element of control and choice in their lives, for example over who they wish to act on their behalf, spend their leisure time with or turn to in times of distress or uncertainty. In some hard pressed local authorities, practical and administrative reasons may hamper social workers from working directly with young people. However, the research studies suggest that equally relevant is the lack of knowledge, confidence and skills necessary to undertake this work. Unlike child protection work, once social workers qualify there are few additional training opportunities or practice guides for working with adolescents.

3. Main findings and their implications for policy and practice

This overview examines the over-arching themes arising from the three studies and explores their meaning for social work policy and practice. The research authors have described in detail the implications from their particular research and the reader is advised to refer to these for specific recommendations.

The research was unequivocal in showing that life was grim for the majority of teenagers in need of social work services. Most were disadvantaged in many areas of life, such as poor or non-existent relationships with family, disjointed schooling, unstable living situations, low self-esteem and poor social skills. For the majority of young people the research shows outcomes a year on were relatively positive. However, when social work services failed to ameliorate existing problems or prevent them from escalating, the combination of deficits hampered young people's transition to adult living. Outcomes for these young adults were poor and many teenagers were prone to acute loneliness and depression, anti-social behaviour such as drug or alcohol abuse, early parenthood, a lack of qualifications, poor job opportunities and homelessness.

A policy for teenagers

The range of problems facing this group of young people and their families qualifies them for services under Part III of the Children Act 1989. At present much service provision is targeted at child protection and families with young children. The research has shown that adolescents are also 'children in need'.

To address the needs of adolescents and their families local authority social services departments must first focus more attention on families with adolescents. There is a need for a coherent policy for teenagers because, although the research highlighted many examples of good practice, generally the response of social services and other related agencies was unfocused and piecemeal.

To develop a local authority policy for teenagers will require the corporate approach to service provision stipulated by Section 27 of the Children Act 1989. To accomplish this social services must work alongside education, health and housing, but also additional agencies such as the police, probation, employment, youth services and relevant voluntary bodies. To ensure policies and procedures are 'user friendly' and services are relevant to young people themselves, teenagers must have a voice at all stages of the process.

A policy for teenagers needs to be reinforced by written procedures and practice guidance. These should identify the services available to young people, lay down procedures for ensuring a joint agency approach, and make sure services are monitored and undergo regular review. A policy for teenagers must be sufficiently flexible to take account of the needs of different groups, such as those from particular cultural or religious backgrounds, young parents, or those with physical and learning disabilities.

When young people move towards independence many fail to negotiate or co-ordinate their requirements with the various agencies, such as social work, employment, health, social security and housing. A policy for teenagers needs to provide for the co-ordination of the different services and nominate a particular agency or care manager to be responsible for overall service provision.

The Order requiring Local Authorities to plan services for children will be of special significance for teenagers, particularly those moving into adulthood. Many agencies are significant in the lives of teenagers. Some play a crucial role. Young people making direct contact on their own, maybe for the first time, with an agency will be greatly helped if the response they can expect is part of a co-ordinated strategy which reflects agreed shared objectives for promoting their well-being.

Supportive services

Local authorities might pursue a preventative strategy indirectly, through support and collaboration with independently run voluntary projects for teenagers. In addition, a more direct response for services could be offered to the smaller number of families and young people such as those facing severe problems over health and relationships.

The recent initiative of using a single venue, such as the family centre or primary school, to co-ordinate services for families with young children offers a useful model for bringing together service provision for adolescents. Local authorities need to identify or expand similarly accessible and non-stigmatising venues. A network of 'drop-in' centres, operating an open door policy would allow all families or carers with troubled or troublesome teenagers, as well as young adults who have ceased to be 'looked after', to easily obtain help and support.

Assessment and planning

The research has shown that a simple model of need assessment, followed by delivery of services was not always the most suitable method when working with adolescents. Assessments need to be flexible because teenagers are likely to change their minds and are influenced in what they do by people and events over which social workers have little control. If teenagers do not perceive the assessment as relevant or if the services are not quickly forthcoming, they are likely to take the initiative into their own hands. Social work assessments need to take into account the complex cycle of assessment, negotiation, changing circumstances, reassessment and revision of plans.

'Multiplex' placements

Traditionally a placement was seen as a single entity with the emphasis on bringing back stability into young people's lives. Whilst successful for those who achieved and enjoyed this stability, for many teenagers this resulted in a series of linear placements where every change increased their sense of rejection and failure. Assessment and planning need to explore both current and anticipated placement requirements and be sufficiently flexible to allow for young people's changing circumstances.

To achieve this, a placement might incorporate a number of 'known' contexts, all or most of which are based within the local community. This would allow resources to be pooled and responsibility and knowledge about the young person to be shared rather than lost, as frequently occurs under the present system. Such a 'multiplex' placement would have built-in flexibility and ensure necessary moves are between a set of previously identified options. This type of placement would allow other aspects of young people's lives, such as schooling or friendship patterns, to remain intact. A 'multiplex' approach would also enable accepted and understood returns to, for example, birth parents, carers or boarding schools, when things cooled down and bridges had been mended.

Such a flexible approach to young people is also needed once young people are no longer 'looked after'. A partnership between social services, leaving care schemes and housing, can facilitate a range of housing possibilities and help young care leavers find and sustain suitable accommodation. Local authorities need to pursue joint initiatives and encourage greater provision of transitional forms of accommodation. A range of supported hostels and lodgings should help prepare care leavers not yet ready for independence and offer a second chance to those facing homelessness.

Direct work with young people and families

Present practice indicates that a constant fear of child abuse scandals determines the use of limited resources and results in many social workers acting primarily as resource managers when cases involve teenagers. Social services departments need to urgently reconsider the current balance in their work between child protection and services for young people. Greater emphasis needs to be placed on direct work with teenagers and families, in particular on training social workers in the use of mediation skills and conflict resolution. The research showed that when relationships between teenagers and their families were poor, social workers who applied these skills were frequently very effective in bringing about some degree of rapprochement.

A champion

In order for teenagers in need of social work services to fulfil their potential and gain the most from the opportunities available, a consistent adult must act as their champion. Included in the range of duties inherent in such a role would be negotiating with officials and other agencies for the most appropriate services, enabling the young person's views to be heard, and making sure agreed decisions are implemented. The Children Act 1989 recognised this need and extended the responsibility to advise, assist and befriend, to young adults up to 21 who are no longer 'looked after'. Local authorities need to ensure that teenagers in their care, as well as young adults who cease to be 'looked after' have a designated worker – a champion – committed to promoting their well being.

A mentor

When relationships between young people and their families had irretrievably broken down, many teenagers found themselves isolated and had no-one to whom they could turn for advice or help. Social services need to provide teenagers with a professional whom they can trust, who is not afraid to discuss sensitive topics, and who is prepared to persevere in the face of the young person's minor transgressions. However, to ensure social workers have the necessary knowledge, skills and support to work on fundamental issues with young people has resource implications, but the alternative of doing nothing can result in far greater costs.

Trust and respect depends on the dynamics inherent in individual relationships. Local authorities need to make explicit that teenagers are given some choice over which professional they wish to develop their main relationship with. Policy formulation must allow either field workers, key workers or foster carers to assume this role, and when young people leave care, the continued use of carers as 'out-reach' workers.

Health

The research showed that delivering health care to teenagers was not easy. Attempts were hampered because social workers and health professionals frequently worked to different time scales, and/or young people and their families believed the checks and tests to be largely irrelevant and therefore failed to co-operate. Local authority social services departments need to negotiate with Health Authorities and Trusts the services they want for children and young people in their care.

Education

When teenagers who are settled in a particular school need to be 'looked after', it is essential, not only for their academic career but also for their emotional and social well-being, that the care plan allows them to remain there.

Many teenagers 'looked after' enter the system with a history of behavioural and educational problems. Social Services Departments in conjunction with Local Education Authorities and individual schools, need to develop an early warning system without negative labelling, so speedy intervention can prevent school related problems escalating.

When teenagers are no longer being educated, either because they have 'opted out' or been permanently excluded, social services need to continue to hold the notion of 'keeping young people learning' as a prime target when planning packages of care. In considering alternative provision, attention needs to be paid to the aspects of residential schools shown by the research to be associated with better outcome, that is their regime and atmosphere, orientation towards achievable goals, smaller classes, and high levels of pastoral care.

Identity

Young people who remained confused about their past also lacked self-esteem and were less confident and assertive. Emphasis needs to be placed on continuing appropriate links with parents, siblings and wider kin because, even when not particularly harmonious, in most cases they were found to have an important symbolic function.

Practical and social skill preparation

The degree to which young adults, no longer 'looked after', coped with living independently was associated with their age, gender and the amount of practical and social skill preparation they received. Life skills need to be a major element in the assessment of teenagers, form an important part of the through-care plan and be subject to a review process. Foster carers and residential workers need guidance and training to develop individual programmes of preparation for the young people they look after. In particular there is a need to review expectations and practice when working with teenage boys. When young people live in residential care it is important they are given the opportunities which family homes more readily offer, to take risks and be involved in decision making.

Young people who ceased to be 'looked after' at 16 were particularly vulnerable to poor outcomes. Assessment at the leaving stage is necessary to secure an appropriate balance between gate-keeping valuable services while targeting those at greatest risk. The fragility of some young care leavers' lives means continuing professional support will be a necessity. Serious consideration needs to be given to ensuring that the most vulnerable young people are identified and 'looked after' for longer – at least until the age of 18. On leaving they may also require greater support than the majority of teenage care leavers and the opportunity to return to a known 'safe' context if they fail to cope.

A supportive framework for carers and social workers

The reader will recall that this overview utilised the criteria developed by Parker and colleagues to assess the progress of 'children looked after' (Parker et al., 1991; Ward, 1995). This work generated the 'Looking After Children Assessment and Action Records' to help carers and social workers address the developmental needs of children and teenagers (Dartington Social Research Unit, 1995). These instruments have been widely tested, and since the completion of these three studies some 72 local authorities have introduced them. The 'records' address the deficits and problems highlighted by the current research but more importantly focus on achievements and set goals. Although they will prove invaluable for assessing and monitoring the progress of children 'looked after' the instability inherent in many teenagers' lives might make them appear less practical. Nonetheless, their framework provides an excellent tool with which to engage with teenagers to jointly assess their health, education and development. Furthermore, even if the process is interrupted by moments of non co-operation or periods of absence, they will enable professionals to monitor the young person's progress and continue important developmental work, or arrange appropriate services, when circumstances allow.

The way forward – Planning Children's Services

To effect strategic change in the implementation of local authority policies, all social work activity, and that of other agencies, needs to be firmly rooted in Children's Services Plans which are jointly conceived and owned by different departments. An Order making planning children's services a mandatory activity of social services departments was implemented on 1 April 1996 accompanied by guidance issued jointly by the Department of Health and the Department for Education and Employment, and distributed by the Home Office and the National Health Services Management Executive. This stresses the importance of co-operation and joint planning. Only by rationalising resources across agencies and recognising how services are best accepted by teenagers will there be health, education and personal social services which are attuned to their multi-faceted needs. Such an approach would ensure that all teenagers, but expressly those who are, or have been, looked after by a local authority, are given every opportunity to make a successful transition to adulthood.

4. References

Aldgate, J., Maluccio, A. and Reeves, C. (1989) *Adolescents in Foster Families*, London, Batsford.

Aldgate, J., Heath, A., Colton, M. and Simon, M. (1993) 'Social work and the education of children in foster care', *Adoption and Fostering*, 17, pp.25–34.

Baker, O., Marsden, J. (1994) *Drug Misuse in Britain*, London, ISDD.

Balding, J. (1995) *Young People in 1994: the health-related behaviour questionnaire results for 48,297 pupils between 11 and 16*, Schools Health Education Unit, University of Exeter.

Bandura, A. (1990) 'Perceived self-efficacy in the exercise of control over AIDS infection', *Evaluation and Programme Planning*, 13, pp.9–17.

Banks, M., Bates, I., Breakwell, G., Bynner, J., Emler, W., Jamieson, L. and Roberts, K. (1992) *Careers and Identities*, Buckingham, Open University Press.

Berridge, D. (1985) *Children's Homes*, Oxford, Blackwell.

Berridge, D. and Cleaver, H. (1987) *Foster Home Breakdown*, Oxford, Blackwell.

Biehal, N., Clayden, J., Stein, M. and Wade, J. (1995) *Moving On: Young People and Leaving Care Schemes*, London, HMSO.

Bullock, R., Little, M. and Millham, S. (1994) 'Assessing the quality of life for children in local authority care or accommodation', *Journal of Adolescence*, 17, pp.29–40.

Children Act 1989 (Amendment) (Children's Services Planning) Order 1996, Statutory Instrument 1996 No. 785.

Cleaver, H. (forthcoming) 'Following study of Vulnerable Children in Schools', *Report submitted to the Department for Education and Employment*.

Cleaver, H. and Freeman, P. (1995) *Parental Perspectives in Cases of Suspected Child Abuse*, London, HMSO.

Coleman, J.C. and Hendry, L. (1990) *The Nature of Adolescence*, London, Routledge, Chapman and Hall.

Collins, W.A. (1990) 'Parent child relationships in the transition to adolescence: continuity and change in interaction effect and cognition', in Montemayor, R., Adams, G.R. and Gullotta, T. (Eds.) *Advances in Adolescent Development, Vol. 11: The Transition from Childhood to Adolescence: A Transitional Period?*, Newbury Park, CA: Sage.

Dartington Social Research Unit (1995) *Looking After Children: Assessment and Action Records (Revised Version)*, London, HMSO.

Department for Education (1993) *A New Deal for 'Out of School' Pupils*, Press Release, 126/93.

Department for Education and Department of Health (1994a) *Pupils with Problems:* Circulars, DfE.

Department for Education and Department of Health (1994b) *The Education of Children being looked after by Local Authorities*, Circular number 13/94, DFE.

Department of Health (1985) *Social Work Decisions in Child Care*, London, HMSO.

Department of Health (1991) *Patterns and Outcomes in Child Placement: Messages from Current Research and their Implications*, London, HMSO.

Department of Health (1995) *Child Protection: Messages from Research*, London, HMSO.

Family Rights Group, (1991) *The Children Act 1989: Working in Partnership with Families*, London, HMSO.

Farrington, D.P. (1980) 'Truancy, delinquency, the home and the school', in Hersov, L. and Berg, I. (Eds.) *Out of School*, Chichester, John Wiley.

Farrington, D.P. (1990) 'Age, period, cohort and offending', in Gottfredson, D.M. and Clarke, R.V. (Eds.) *Policy and Theory in Criminal Justice*, Aldershot, Hants, Avebury.

Farrington, D.P. (1991) 'Anti-social personality from childhood to adulthood', *The Psychologist*, 4, 9, pp.289–394.

Fisher, M., Marsh, P., Phillips, D. and Sainsbury, E. (1986) *In and Out of Care: the Experiences of Children, Parents and Social Workers*, Batsford in association with the British Agencies for Adoption and Fostering.

Fletcher-Campbell, F. and Hall, C. (1991) *Changing Schools? Changing People? A Study of the Education of Children in Care*, Berkshire, NFER-Nelson.

Harris, R. and Timms, N. (1993) *Secure Accommodation in Child Care*, London, Routledge.

Hibbert, A., Fogelman, K. and Manor, O. (1990) 'Occupational outcomes of truancy', *British Journal of Educational Psychology*, 60, pp.23–36.

Jackson, S. (1989) 'Residential care and education', *Children and Society,* 4, pp.335–50.

Kahan, B. (1980) *Growing Up in Care*, Oxford, Blackwell.

Kay, H. (1994) *Conflicting Priorities*, London, CHAR and the Institute of Housing.

Lambert, L. (1983) *A Study of the Health of Children in Care using Information Derived from the National Child Development Study*, National Children's Bureau Report to the Social Science Research Council.

Lambert, R. with Millham, S. (1968) *The Hothouse Society*, London, Weidenfeld and Nicolson.

Leffert, N. and Petersen, A.C. (1995) 'Patterns of development in adolescence', in Rutter, M. and Smith, D.J. (Eds.) *Psycho-social Disorders in Young People: Time Trends and their Causes*, Chichester, Wiley.

Local Authority Circular LAC (96) 10 Children's Services Planning.

Magnusson, D. and Bergman, L. (1990) 'A pattern approach to the study of pathways from childhood to adulthood', in Robins, L. and Rutter, M. (Eds.) *Straight and Devious Pathways from Childhood to Adulthood*, New York, Cambridge University Press.

Millham, S., Bullock, R. and Hosie, K. (1978) *Locking up Children*, Farnborough, Saxon House.

Millham, S., Bullock, R., Hosie, K. and Haak, M. (1981) *Issues of Control in Residential Child Care,* London, HMSO.

Millham, S., Bullock, R., Hosie, K. and Haak, M. (1986) *Lost in Care*, Dorset, Blackmore.

OPCS (1995) *General Household Survey 1993*, London, HMSO.

Packman, J. with Randall, J. and Jacques, N. (1986) *Who Needs Care?,* Oxford, Blackwell.

Packman, J. and Hall, C. (1995) *Draft Report on the Implementation of Section 20 of the Children Act, 1989*, Dartington Social Research Unit.

Parker, R., Ward, H., Jackson, S., Aldgate, J. and Wedge, P. (1991) *Looking After Children: Assessing Outcomes in Child Care*, London, HMSO.

Page, R. and Clark, G. (1977) *Who Cares*, London, National Children's Bureau.

Refugee Council (1995) *Government Social Security Proposals: Refugee Council Briefing,* October 1995.

Robins, L. (1978) 'Study of childhood predictors of adult anti-social behaviour: Replications from longitudinal studies', *Psychological Medicine*, 8, pp.611–22.

Robins, L. (1986) 'The consequences of conduct disorders in girls', in Olwins, D., Black, J. and Radke-Yarrow, M. (Eds.) *Development of Anti-social and Pro-social Behaviour: Research Theories and Issues*, New York, Academic Press.

Rutter, M. (1985) 'Family and school influences: meanings, mechanisms and implications', in Nicol, R.A. (Ed.) *Longitudinal Studies in Child Psychology and Psychiatry*, London, Wiley and Sons.

Rutter, M. (1990) 'Changing patterns of psychiatric disorders during adolescence' in Bancroft, J. and Reinisch, D.M. (Eds.) *Adolescence and Puberty*, New York, Oxford University Press.

Rutter, M., Tizard, J. and Whitmore, K. (Eds.) (1970) *Education, Health and Behaviour*, London, Longman.

Rutter, M., Graham, P., Chadwick, O.F.D. and Yule, W. (1976) 'Adolescent Turmoil: Fact or Fiction?', *Journal of Child Psychology and Psychiatry*, 17, pp.35-56.

Seden, J. (1995) 'Religious persuasion and the Children Act', *Adoption and Fostering*, 19, 2, pp.7–15.

Sinclair, R., Garnett, L. and Berridge, D. (1995) *Social Work and Assessment with Adolescents*, London, National Children's Bureau.

Small, J. (1986) 'Transracial placements: conflicts and contradictions', in Ahmed, S., Cheetham, J. and Small, J. (Eds.) *Social Work with Black Children and their Families,* London, Batsford.

Social Services Inspectorate, (1985) *The Inspection of Community Homes,* London, HMSO.

Social Services Inspectorate, (1991) *Children in the Public Care*, London, HMSO.

Social Services Inspectorate and OFSTED, (1995) *The Education of Children Who are Looked After by Local Authorities*, Department of Health and OFSTED.

Stein, M. and Carey, K. (1986) *Leaving Care*, Oxford, Blackwell.

Tizard, B. and Phoenix, A. (1993) *Black, White or Mixed Race?, Race and Racism in the Lives of Young People of Mixed Parentage,* London, Routledge.

Tizard, B. and Phoenix, A. (1995) 'The identity of mixed parentage adolescents', *Journal of Child Psychology and Psychiatry*, 36, 8, pp.1399–1410.

Triseliotis, J., Borland, M., Hill, M. and Lambert, L. (1995) *Teenagers and the Social Work Services*, London, HMSO.

Tutt, N. (1974) *Care or Custody?*, London, Dart, Longman and Todd.

Ward, H. (Ed.) (1995) *Looking After Children: Research into Practice, the Second Report to the Department of Health on Assessing Outcomes in Child Care*, London, HMSO.

Weiner, A. and Weiner, E. (1990) *Expanding the Options in Child Placement: Israel's Dependent Children in Care from Infancy to Adulthood*, New York, University Press of America.

Zoccolillo, M., Pickles, A., Quinton, D. and Rutter, M. (1992) 'The outcome of childhood conduct disorder: Implications for defining adult personality disorder and conduct disorder', *Psychological Medicine*, 22, pp.971–86.

Summaries

Social Work and Assessment with Adolescents

Ruth Sinclair, Louise Garnett and David Berridge

The aims of the research

The overall aim of this study was to compare the characteristics of different forms of assessment in social work with adolescents and to ascertain whether these led to different outcomes for the young people. The research addressed questions such as – how are young people allocated to different assessments; how do these assessments vary in their procedures and practices; who participates; how do the participants perceive the assessment process; what are the results from the assessment; what are the relative costs of the various assessment packages; is there a relationship between costs and outcomes in terms of the child's subsequent care career; what is the outcome of these assessments in terms of their impact on the young person's circumstances one year on?

The design of the study

The research was conducted in one local authority which had access to a range of assessment facilities. Assessments were categorised as *routine* or *referred*: routine assessments were those undertaken by social workers as part of their normal case responsibilities; referred assessments were carried out by specialist assessment workers. Within both categories the assessment could take place while the young person was in residential care, foster care or living in the community with family and friends. Both assessment types were also likely to involve professionals from other agencies.

The definition of assessment employed in the study was *'a significant preparation for decision-making, typically occurring at a point of transition in the child's care career'*. Young people included in the sample had undergone an assessment following one of three events – the young person was at risk of being accommodated, they had become looked after, or they had experienced a placement breakdown.

Information was gathered from files and social work interviews three months after the assessment commenced and again a year later. Interviews were also conducted with young people, parents, carers, managers and other professionals.

The young people

Seventy five young people were included in the sample, 41 boys and 34 girls. Although their ages ranged from 10 to 17, over two-thirds of the group were aged 14 to 16. The sample represented great ethnic diversity, with almost two-thirds coming from black or minority ethnic groups. Eight of the young people were unaccompanied refugees. Although a few of the young people had experienced abuse the major concerns at the time of the assessment related to family relationships, behaviour and school-related problems.

Research findings

This study tells us much about the nature of social work with adolescents, the complexities of that task, the challenges and the successes. Here we summarise just some of these findings under 3 headings; the assessment process, social work with adolescents, and the outcomes for young people.

The assessment process

Although there were major differences in the assessment procedures – 'referred' assessments were undertaken in a more systematic way with clear timescales and procedures for involving young people – the outputs from both types of assessment indicated similar problems in completing assessment and constructing comprehensive care plans. Less than half of the assessments were completed fully or in most respects within the 3 months timescale; although plans were made in respect of all the young people there were significant gaps, especially in relation to education and issues of identity.

Referred assessments were considerably more expensive than routine assessments. However, this is largely because these assessments are more likely to be residential, and accommodation was the largest cost factor in the assessment packages. However, the study does suggest that the costs of assessments were related to the needs of the young people, although the links between costs and outcomes was somewhat more tenuous.

Despite ready access to professionals in other agencies, the multi-disciplinary nature of assessments was a major stumbling block to successful completion. In particular, differences in the pace and timescale between professionals and the effort required to co-ordinate assessments led to difficulties for social workers. This study highlights the changes necessary in the relationship between professionals in social services and other agencies if the wide ranging needs of these adolescents are to be met.

The study points to a lack of any single concept or common understanding of what is meant by assessment, with increasing fragmentation in child care planning as assessment with different purposes are undertaken under separate procedures. Could this be avoided by the development of integrated assessment and planning systems applied in a way that allows for variation in the process depending on the particular purposes of any one assessment?

Social work with adolescents

Engaging with young people: Social work intervention with adolescents is unlikely to be successful unless someone – social worker, carer, or other professional – is able to actively engage with the young person and to relate to them in a meaningful way. There was much evidence throughout this study of the failure to achieve this level of engagement – and the positive outcomes when this did occur. The level of contact between social workers and young people was surprisingly low. Decision-making and resource management seem to be accorded higher priority than working with young people and their families; as direct work with young people has become devalued so social workers have become less skilled in this area. Difficulties in engaging with young people were apparent with other professionals; for instance referrals to family therapy, or psychiatric services rarely led to a sustained programme of work.

Working with parents: Similarly this study suggests that parents received little attention, social workers had even less contact with parents than with young people. If partnership with parents is to have any meaning when working with adolescents then such work must be given higher priority and social workers equipped to undertake work with parents.

Ethnicity: The young people receiving services from the 'research' authority come from a great diversity of ethnic backgrounds and undoubtedly this posed some challenges. This highlights the importance of taking account of all four components of ethnicity – 'religious persuasion, racial origin, cultural and linguistic background'. The heterogeneity of the population makes placement 'matching' a complex task. It certainly means that in assessment and care planning generalised assumptions must be replaced by specific knowledge relating to each individual child.

Adolescents as a client group: This study points to the low priority that is accorded social work with adolescents. The emphasis given to child protection in terms of time, resources, the allocation of experienced and skilled staff has real consequences for these 'teenagers in need'.

Outcomes

A range of measures was used to assess the outcomes for young people one year on. Inevitably the outcomes for the group show a degree of variation; some were noticeably more settled but for a few there were significant needs which had not been met. However, overall the picture was relatively positive.

There were some major gaps in the plans made following assessment and only limited success in implementing them – particularly in securing long-term foster homes and suitable education. Undoubtedly some of the positive outcomes could be said to be despite social work intervention rather than because of it. Moreover social workers were seen as being more successful in meeting the material needs of the young people – somewhere to live, a source of income, – rather than their emotional needs.

A key finding from the study was that the outcomes for the young people did not differ significantly with assessment type. For these young people the quality of the social work input was more important than specific assessment procedures. This study points to four factors which appear to be associated with successful implementation of social work decision and better outcomes for young people these are:-

- continuing input from a social worker, ideally allocation of the same social worker;

- persistence by the social worker in working on behalf of the young person;

- an ability by social workers or others to actively engage with the young person and to undertake direct work with them;

- a lack of dependence by social workers on input from other professionals.

This suggests that the value of assessment and planning will be limited if it is not supported by sufficient high quality social work input, especially working directly with young people to address their specific needs.

Teenagers and the Social Work Services

John Triseliotis, Moira Borland, Malcolm Hill and Lydia Lambert

Summary of key findings

The main aims of this study were to examine programmes of care and supervision for teenagers who become subject to social services intervention. It was important to single out this age group because of the scant attention paid to them previously, except in relation to specific issues like offending or leaving care. The researchers investigated the range of child care policies, services and practice in five social services and social work departments in order to understand how these impinged on the needs and problems of teenagers and their families.

The study was planed on a longitudinal basis over one year in order to compare initial expectations with resource deployment and later achievements and in order to trace progress following intervention. A sample was identified of 116 teenagers aged 13–17 who were experiencing the start of a new form of social services intervention or a significant change in care or supervision arrangements. Participants in the study were recruited from 3 local authorities in England and two in Scotland. The study was carried out between 1991 and 1993.

The main part of the research consisted of initial and follow-up interviews approximately one year apart with the young person, social worker and parents in each case, except when a potential respondent was unavailable or unwilling to be seen. The measures of progress included standardised Rutter and Coopersmith scales, which assess psychosocial development and self-esteem respectively.

Sample characteristics

At the start of the study, about three fifths of the sample were living away from home, mostly 'accommodated', though a few were already living 'independently'. The remainder were being supervised at home – on a court order (in England), under a supervision requirement by the Hearing (in Scotland) or informally as a preventive measure.

The young people were clearly a difficult population, with nine out of ten scoring above the normal cut-off point on the Rutter scale. Most had a history of poor schooling and many had low self-esteem. Only a minority were from intact two parent households. Attitudinal and relationship difficulties were often compounded by financial and environmental stresses, though not invariably.

Problems, needs and expectations

Social workers became involved with the teenagers and their families for three main reasons:

- disputes and conflicts between the teenager and parents(s) or step parent;

- school-related problems, especially non-attendance;

- offending and/or involvement in drug, solvent or alcohol abuse.

The most typical pattern was for a cluster of family-school-behaviour problems to be present. In contrast to parents, social workers tended to underplay undesirable behaviours and the intensity of family conflict. Whilst a few teenagers in the study had been seriously abused, usually child protection issues did not feature.

In the absence of specific policies and strategies, social workers were often unsure how to respond to requests for voluntary help and the opportunity for early preventive intervention was consequently delayed to the disappointment of the parents. Compulsory measures were sometimes suggested to parents to ensure access to service provision.

Parents, social workers and the young people did not always see problems and needs in the same way and hence framed their desired solutions differently. Young people set expectations largely in terms of immediate practical concerns and preoccupations, whilst parents put most emphasis on behavioural changes. In contrast, practitioners were more likely to formulate goals based on the perceived longer term needs of the young person, such as increased confidence, maturity and self-esteem.

Available support and the range of services offered

Following intervention, social workers and their agencies brought into play a wide range of services. Their availability varied from one agency to another and also within the agencies. In particular, foster care, group work and outreach were much easier to gain access to in some areas than others, even within the same authority. The same was also true about consistent individual and family work. Similarly, supervision at home took highly variable forms, according to the nature of the identified problems, the services available locally or the approach of the particular social worker. Consequently allocation of services resulted as much from local provision and custom as from young people's needs or preferences. Yet better outcomes were usually related to the consistent deployment of a range of resources than to single forms of intervention.

Many of the placements in care were short-lived, a matter of weeks or months. Although teenagers may be more able to adapt to changes than younger children, the placement turnover during the year left cause for concern reinforcing the instability already experienced by many young people in their family lives.

Consumers' views of social work intervention

The majority of the teenagers were positive about the social work intervention, but fewer thought it had a major impact on their lives. We encountered a minority who were disenchanted with most adults and resented efforts to control their behaviour, but these were the exception. Even this minority usually had at least one adult they trusted and respected – a parent, teacher, group worker, key worker or social worker. Generally social workers were well liked, but this liking of social workers did not necessarily go with positive change. Most of the teenagers reacted well to professionals and carers when they perceived them as understanding, reliable and active on their behalf.

When the relationship was good and they respected their social worker, the teenagers welcomed straight talking and warnings about the consequences of their behaviour. A surprisingly high proportion in this group claimed this had helped them to reduce or stop offending. Some social workers were able to establish rapport and relationships with very 'disturbed' teenagers as well as less problematic ones.

In spite of the frustration expressed by many parents at the absence of consistent preventive services, by the follow-up period more than half said they got on well with the social workers and were broadly favourable about the service. Like their children, they valued the counselling and supportive role as well as practical assistance. However, significantly higher proportions of parents than teenagers complained that the intervention had been ineffective or different from what they wanted.

Perceptions of particular services

Residential Homes/Units. The majority of placements in residential units were considered beneficial and some had provided much needed care at a crucial point. However, residential units were markedly less successful than residential schools in terms of placement stability and feedback from social workers and parents. There was some evidence to suggest that the more troublesome a young person was, the more likely that he or she would be moved around, which only made the situation worse.

Individual residential carers in all types of units were very highly praised by both young people and their parents. The value of placements was enhanced when residential and field work staff understood each other's roles well and worked in tandem to provide effective support to young people and, where appropriate, to their parents. Key workers appeared crucial for many young people and their availability and especially continuity was particularly valued.

Residential Schools. These proved to be the most popular and durable of the three main placement types for those who experienced them. Young people with a long history of discomfort about going to their local school found the environment much more acceptable. Parents, too, were often delighted that their children were receiving education and not roaming the streets. Most residents went home at weekends and contacts with family and friends were maintained. The population of residential schools comprised a high proportion of young people with significant behaviour difficulties so their favourable outcomes could not be attributed to them caring for a less problematic population.

Foster Care was offered to only a minority of the teenagers placed away from home and in one agency was hardly ever considered. Nevertheless, one third of all placements were in foster care. Because of the acute shortage of suitable placements, notions of matching could not be fully applied. Similarly, only a few placements were with carers who were specially trained and supported. These factors may partly account for the fact that foster placements were more likely than residential ones to finish ahead of the planned date and sooner than needed.

After-Care Services. Overall about one fifth of the sample lived on their own or in supported accommodation at some point during the year. Some had set out with high expectations, but were soon disillusioned by mounting debts, unsuitable housing, lack of support, loneliness and the uncertainties of the benefits system. Often they found it hard to deal with the various agencies which might help with money, work, education or housing and some gave up. This was the most vulnerable, unhappy and dissatisfied group of young people from amongst the whole sample. Several felt that the 'system' wanted to get rid of them before they were ready.

Home-based Supervision. Social workers sometimes seemed uncertain how to tackle the dual tasks of modifying the young people's behaviour (usually offending) and improving their welfare. Some social workers were not happy or comfortable having to supervise unmotivated and unco-operative youngsters, but in a number of cases barriers were overcome and trust established by a combination of friendly informality and direct action (e.g. advocacy). About a fifth of young people seemed to benefit a lot from home supervision, with many of the initial problems reduced or stopped. In Chapter 6 of the main publication the components are outlined of the policy, practice and resources required to make supervision more effective.

Group Work and Befriending. The study showed that meetings with peers and individualised attention from a 'friendly' adult could take many forms and be adapted to children both at home and away from home. Usually this kind of help was well liked by the teenagers, although both they and the social workers were more circumspect about how much effect it had on the initial problems.

Participation in decision-making

The agencies in the study had clear policies stressing co-operation and joint planning with parents and young people. More parents than young people had been in favour of supervision or care. Subsequently, the position reversed and parents were more likely to feel that they had little influence on placement choice and were not kept informed of plans or developments. Most young people felt they had been consulted about later decisions and that they were adequately prepared for moves. However, participation in decision-making was hampered by limited choices, ignorance about options and lack of skills in expressing themselves or negotiating with adults.

The majority of the teenagers were reasonably happy with child care reviews. Either they felt well able to speak for themselves or else they were confident that social workers, key workers or parents would get their views across. There was some resentment at having too many adults present, especially people they knew hardly or not at all. Preparatory talk with social workers and key workers seemed to be helpful. Fewer were confident about speaking in court or at a panel.

Changes and overall progress

More than two thirds of the young people had concluded that overall their lives were better at the end of the year than at the start, albeit not always in their view because of social work intervention. However, this applied to only one third of those living independently. Good progress occurred in a wide range of circumstances and was not confined to easier cases nor closely linked to particular types of problem or intervention. Getting on well with the social worker did not necessarily lead to a reduction in problems, but there was some association between a good relationship and overall success.

Looking for positive outcomes in relation to stated expectations and needs a year earlier, proved complex, elusive and fraught with difficulties. This was mainly because objectives had not been properly agreed, each party had a different perspective and expectations also tended to shift. Continued reviewing and redefinition was therefore required and this had seldom happened.

Packages of services

The main study outlines tentative conclusions about the kind of packages of services that worked well. The most successful service package usually involved a combination of complementary input which included a sensitive but firm approach from professionals and/or carers based on clear joint planning with the young person or family. The diversity of circumstances emphasised the need for a wide range of services to be available.

Moving On: Young People and Leaving Care Schemes

Nina Biehal, Jasmine Clayden, Mike Stein and Jim Wade

Research aims and methods

The main purpose of our study was to investigate different leaving care schemes and approaches to leaving care. The setting up of the first specialist schemes in the mid-1980's and the development of different models by statutory and voluntary agencies raised key questions which our research set out to explore. First, what different scheme models and approaches to leaving care were developing and what services did they provide? Second, how effective were different schemes, particularly in relation to outcomes for young people? Finally, how did the outcomes and experiences of young people using schemes compare to those not being assisted by schemes?

To answer these questions we planned a two stage study. We began with a survey of patterns of leaving care in our three different English local authorities – City, County and District. Information was collected by social worker completed questionnaire in respect of 183 young people aged 16–19 who left care during a six month period. This was complemented by our longitudinal and in-depth qualitative study of the process of leaving care and the support offered to care leavers by the four leaving care schemes in our three authorities. Our qualitative sample totalled 74 young people, being comprised of a 'participating' group who received key worker support from the schemes and a 'comparison group' of non-scheme young people. These young people, their social workers and, where applicable their scheme workers, were interviewed after the young person left care and on two subsequent occasions during an 18–24 month period. By this method we were able to chart their experiences during their transition from care to living in the community. What were the characteristics of these young people who participated in our follow-up study?

Profile of the study

The 74 young people in the qualitative sample were all aged 16–19 when recruited to the research and of these 39% were male and 61% female. The majority of the sample (88%) were white although nine black or mixed heritage young people (12%) participated. Six young people (8%) were considered to have special support needs, five with learning difficulties and one with a serious mental health problem. Over half (56%) had entered care as teenagers, but two fifths had been accommodated for ten years or more and a further 26% for between four and nine years. Many had experienced a high degree of movement and disruption during the time they were 'looked after'. A third of the sample had made four or more moves during their career, only 16% having remained in the same placement throughout. 41% left care from residential placements and slightly more (45%) from foster care. Only 15% left care from placements with parents or relatives. The majority of our sample were therefore those for whom a return home was not an immediate or realistic option. Over two thirds (69%) of our young people had spent four or more years in substitute care or accommodation and most were thus dependent on social services to equip, prepare and support them in their key transition to adulthood. How did they do? What did we find out about their experiences, the help they received from our schemes and the related outcomes?

Moving on

Young people continue to leave care at a much earlier age than other young people leave home. Nearly two thirds of our young people left before they were 18 and a quarter did so at just 16 years. Some of these young people's foster and residential placements broke down, precipitating a rapid move out of care. But for others there was the assumption that they should move on having reached 16 or 17 years. Where did they go to? Just under half of the group (47%) moved to transitional forms of accommodation such as hostels, lodgings and stays with friends. And for some of these young people who were not yet ready for independent accommodation this proved to be helpful preparation. A fifth (20%) moved to independent tenancies in the public, voluntary or private sector when they first left care and this figure rose to 59% 18–24 months later. Most of these young people needed ongoing support to sustain their tenancies. But lack of preparation, coping with new freedoms and loneliness led to some subsequently losing or leaving their tenancies. Only a small number of our sample (15%) made no move, remaining initially with parents, relatives or foster carers when they ceased to be 'looked after'. And an even smaller number of young people (12%) returned to live with parents or relatives.

For many of these young people their first two years out of care were marked by movement and instability, with over half making two or more moves and a sixth making five or more moves, including planned moves. Just over one fifth (22%) became homeless at some stage.

How well were they prepared practically? Most of our young people had good practical skills at the point of leaving care although less than half of the total sample had good budgeting skills. But fewer were able to acquire these skills gradually from a stable and supportive platform with an opportunity to participate in decision making. Also, constraints in residential care often meant that life skills training became very practically focused and concentrated at the later end of a young person's care career, and this was separated from their emotional development.

Our four leaving care schemes all played a major part in this 'moving on' process. This included planning transitions, preparing young people, providing follow-up support and meeting accommodation needs. In relation to accommodation, our schemes between them were offering directly managed accommodation in trainer flats or specialist hostels, 'floating support schemes', arranging access to supported lodgings or hostels provided by other agencies and arranging and supporting young people in independent tenancies. Even for those young people experiencing the greatest instability, continuity of support by schemes often prevented a descent into homelessness or provided a rapid escape from it. Our analysis of accommodation outcomes showed that not only were leaving care schemes working with those who had the most unstable early housing careers but also that they were able to help the vast majority find good accommodation within two years.

Education and career paths

For the majority of our young people care was unable to compensate them for their damaging pre-care experiences and thus establish a successful pattern of schooling. Over half the young people we spoke to had left school with no qualifications and only three had attained three or more GCSE's at grade A-C. For a significant minority care compounded their educational difficulties. The effects of movement, labelling, just 'feeling different' and of patterns of truancy all had a negative impact on their education and future careers on leaving school. Half of our young people were unemployed within a few months of leaving care and nearly two thirds failed to establish a stable career pattern, facing periods of short-term casual work interspersed with episodes of training and unemployment. As a result most of these young people were living on or below benefit levels.

The developmental role of our schemes in promoting education, training and employment was less developed than other areas of their work, although there was evidence of individual careers work and by the end of our research two of our schemes had developed formal links with colleges, career and training agencies. All our schemes had a central role in administering finance for young people and, to varying degrees, in developing and co-ordinating policies including helping authorities discharge their discretionary powers to offer financial assistance under Section 24 funding.

Educational and employment outcomes for all care leavers were very poor compared to the general population. Poor attainment was associated with a high degree of movement while being 'looked after' and better educational attainment was achieved by those whose last placement was in foster care.

Identities and networks

For our young people, the point of leaving care was a time in which many were attempting to make sense of their pasts, to trace missing parents, to find continuity in their lives and a sense of belonging. They needed a 'story' of their lives that made sense, reduced their confusion about both how and why events had happened as they did and to provide a more secure platform for their futures in the adult world. Our findings suggest that those who had retained their family links, even where contact was not very positive, seemed better able to do this. Knowledge of their families, at a minimum, gave a greater symbolic certainty to their lives. Those who remained confused about their pasts found life out of care more difficult to mange – they lacked self-esteem, were less confident and assertive.

There was little perceived difference between our black/mixed heritage and white young people in relation to their degree of self-esteem, knowledge of their background and general sense of purpose. Indeed, the black young people in our study were slightly more likely to have a secure sense of identity, in those terms, than the white young people. For these young people their sense of ethnic identity changed over time and their identification with a particular group was strongly related to their identification with or rejection of family members.

Many of our young people had poor relationships with their families which ruled out a return home. However, family links were very important to most of them, including links with brothers and sisters, grandparents and other members of their extended family. And during our research a third of our young people, representing nearly half of the young women in the sample, had become parents themselves. While over one half of pregnancies had been unplanned over one third were planned at some stage.

Our leaving care schemes were playing only a minimal role in mediating between young people and their families, tending to view this as the social workers' responsibility. But this was not always the case, for fewer than one third of social workers were active in this area once the young person had moved on. When social workers became involved with young parents, whether as a result of child care concerns or not, there was a pervasive tendency to focus on monitoring child care and thus switch their support from mother to child. In contrast, our schemes, when involved, were able to support the mother in her own right.

Our schemes were much more active in helping young people develop friendship networks. Their specialist knowledge of local youth and leisure provision as well as the schemes' own groups and 'drop-in' arrangements were highly valued by young people.

Our outcome analysis reveals the close links between social networks, identities and relationships. Those young people with a secure sense of identity had good or fair social networks and good relationship skills, whereas the majority of those with an insecure sense of identity had poor social networks and poor relationship skills. And most of the young people with a secure sense of identity had positive family relationships.

Leaving care schemes

The contribution of our leaving care schemes in responding to specific needs has been summarised above. More generally, despite their different approaches, we found that they all had made a valuable contribution in assisting their authorities meet their duties and powers under the leaving care sections of the Children Act 1989. Their work had included:

- contributing to policy development and the co-ordination of leaving care services;

- developing a flexible range of resource options, especially housing and financial resources, and co-ordinating access to them;

- developing inter-agency links to ensure an integrated approach;

- providing advice, information and constancy services to young people, social workers and carers – including assistance with preparation and leaving care planning;

- offering direct individual and group based support to young people including both those leaving care and living in the community.

Two final points. Our research set out to investigate different leaving care schemes, so did we find the blueprint for an ideal scheme? The simple answer is 'no.' What we did find out is that to classify any of our four schemes by a single dimension or label would be a gross oversimplification. Our leaving care schemes distinctiveness was derived from differences in perspective, differences in methods of working and, in particular, differences around each scheme's search to find an appropriate balance between 'young person demand led' and 'planned worker led' services; between more reactive open access services and the need for planned pro-active work with young people. Each of our four schemes had different approaches and each had different strengths.

Finally, in reflecting on the 'outcomes' for our young people and by implication the work of the schemes we should continually remind ourselves of where these young people were starting from – the emotional and material deprivation that had blighted their short lives – and recognise, as our research has done, that our schemes achievements, against the odds, were impressive.

Tools, checklists and exercises

All quoted prices exclude VAT, postage and packing.

Alcohol Abuse

Drink Awareness for Youth: An Alcohol Education Resource Pack.
National Youth Council of Ireland, 1991.
Available from: Drink Awareness for Youth, c/o 3 Montague Street, Dublin 2.
£35.00.

Alcohol awareness and education programme designed for those working with young people around alcohol use and abuse. Includes booklets giving factual information on alcohol and a list of suitable games and energisers. The programme itself is made up of a number of units which are designed to provide young people with information on alcohol, an understanding of the influences on them to drink alcohol, and the importance of positive self-image and relationships in their lives.

Teenagers and Alcohol.
John Coleman and Coralie Tiffin, 1993.
Available from: TSA Publishing Ltd., 23 New Road, Brighton, East Sussex, BN1 1WZ. £8.95.

This pack is aimed at parents and all who work with young people. The pack consists of a booklet and an audio cassette tape. Topics include: sensible drinking, the role of parents, alcohol education in school, issues of peer pressure, alcohol, violence and crime, the law relating to alcohol.

Challenging Behaviour

Dealing with Challenging Behaviour: A Barnardo's Guide to Coping with Difficult Young People.
Ivan Sharpe and Clare Gent, 1994.
Available from: Barnardos, Paycocke Road, Basildon, Essex, SS14 3DR. £95.00.

A training book and accompanying video brings together examples of good practice and offers guidance on how to manage challenging behaviour in young people. It is designed to stimulate discussion among staff dealing with difficult young people.

Child Protection

Caring for Children and Young People who have been Sexually Abused.
Linda Croll and Brian Pereira, 1994.
Available from: Breakthrough for Youth, 64 Brendon, Laindon, Essex SS15
5XL. £47.75.

Resource pack for foster carers and residential care workers on working with
children and young people who have been sexually abused. The pack contains a
reader which includes chapters and sessions on aspects of child sex abuse; a
facilitators guide which includes a series of exercises and optional articles; and a
video in which young people talk about their own experiences of sexual abuse.

Working with the Aftermath of Child Sexual Abuse.
Anne Bannister, Carol Dey and Bobbie Print, 1990.
Available from: NSPCC, 33 Gilmour Close, Beaumont Leys, Leicester, LE4
1EZ. £99.00.

A training pack designed to help people who are dealing with all those who may
have been affected by child sexual abuse. It is mainly concerned with therapeutic
issues and the personal consequences for the worker, and is targeted at social
workers, psychologists, psychotherapists, probation officers, residential workers
and workers in voluntary organisations such as Rape Crisis. The pack contains 2
copies of a video on therapeutic techniques, as well as the text.

Child Protection: Messages from Research.
Dartington Social Research Unit, 1995.
Available from: HMSO Publications Centre, PO Box 276, London, SW8 5DT.
£14.00.

Summarises the finding of 20 research studies, this publication explores child
abuse and child protection and seeks to demonstrate the relevance of the findings
for policy and practice. The book is in three parts, of which the third provides
'true for us' exercises for practitioners to identify and compare with their own
cases and working experience.

*Protecting Children in School: A Handbook for Developing Child Protection
Training.*
Jane Wonnacott, 1995.
Available from: National Children's Bureau Enterprises Ltd., 8 Wakley Street,
London, EC1V 7QE. £10.00.

A handbook for those involved in providing child protection training in schools.
It offers a guide to assessing the training needs of staff in school settings, and
identifies readily available materials which can be used in different areas of
training.

🜸 Death

Supporting Bereaved Children and Families.
Cruse, 1993.
Available from: Cruse-Bereavement Care, 126 Sheen Road, Richmond, Surrey, TW9 1UR. £17.99. Running time: 30 minutes.

Manual and accompanying video which aim to assist in the training of bereavement counsellors when counselling bereaved children and their families. Issues covered include the effect of the death of a parent on children and young people, the development of the concept of death in children, and some innovative ways of helping bereaved children, both individually, and as part of a family or peer group. There is also a section on children and disaster.

Disability

Disability Equality in the Classroom: A Human Rights Issue.
Richard Rieser, Inner London Education Authority, 1990.
Available from: Richard Rieser, 23 Walford Road, London, N16 8EF. £10.00.

Detailed wide-ranging thought provoking pack written by disabled people aiming to provide teachers in mainstream and 'special' schools with information on disability issues and thus to affect attitudes and practice. Separate sections look at the politics of disability and ways in which disabled people define their current situation in a prejudiced society, give basic information on disability and guidelines for good practice, and provide detailed examples of how to include disability issues in the national curriculum. A set of worksheets for classroom use is included.

The Disabling Council: A Training Video on Disability Equality.
Local Government Training Board, 1990.
Available from: Local Government Training Board, Arndale House, Arndale Centre, Luton, LU1 2TS. £56.00. Running time: 37 minutes.

Aimed primarily at local authority policy development officers and managers, this video has been produced for use in disability equality training courses. Touching on the real issues of discrimination against disabled people and emphasising that disabled people can be assertive and positive, the video explains how discrimination works in practice, particularly in employment and education, and highlights some approaches that can be used to develop equal opportunities for disabled people. The video is provided with both sign language and subtitles, and a handbook which explains the content and structure of the video and suggests ways in which it could be used.

Drug Abuse

Drugs and the Community: what Local Authorities can do.
Alyson Morley,
Available from: London Drug Policy Forum, The City Secretary's Office, P.O. Box 270, The Guildhall, London, EC2P 2EJ. Free of charge.

Guide produced for local authorities on drug issues. It covers every area of service delivery and aims to set up a framework in which local authorities can develop policies on drug services and prevention.

A Dialogue on Drugs.
Publisher, Nick Ward Production Company, 1994.
Available from: Northumbria Coalition Against Crime, Northumbria Police, Force Headquarters, Ponteland, NE20 OBL. £20.00. Running time 30 mins.

Video pack which consists of a video and support booklet on the subject of drug education with young people. The video presents a group of young people who talk about their experiences of illegal drugs, their availability and effects. It also includes teachers who discuss factors involved in setting up a drug education programme, and drug experts who describe the most commonly used drugs and their prevalence among young people in the North East of England.

Issues of Substance: Information for People Working with Young Drug Users.
Fran Walker, 1994.
Available from: National Children's Bureau, 8 Wakley Street, London, EC1V 7QE. £10.50.

Pack comprising ten cards on different subjects which provide drug workers with essential background information for working with young drug users. Subjects covered include the Children Act 1989, alcohol, solvents and tobacco legislation, confidentiality and consent to treatment, the legal status of drugs, image and provision of information, involving young people and inter-agency co-operation.

Teenagers and Drugs
Dr. John Davies and Niall Coggans of the Addiction Research Group, University of Strathclyde, 1991.
Available from: TSA Publishing Ltd., 23 New Road, Brighton, East Sussex, BN1 1WZ. £8.95.

This pack is aimed at parents and all who work with young people. The pack consists of a booklet and an audio cassette tape. Topics include: the range of drugs available, how to recognise signs of abuse, the role of families, the influence of friends, the types of support available and how to seek advice.

Eating Problems

The Food Mood Guide: A Resource Pack for Work on Food, Feelings and Society for Use with Young Women.
Sheila Ritchie, 1994.
Available from: Youth Clubs UK, 11 St Brides Street, London, EC4A 4AS.
£7.95.

Resource designed for use with groups of young women around the issue of eating problems and the relationship between food, feelings and health. It includes exercises and ideas to promote a better understanding of eating problems, and to encourage young women to feel good about their own body image and help them make their own choices in response to the pressures around them.

Expert Testimony

Expert Testimony: Developing Witness Skills.
David Carson and Ray Bull, 1994.
Available from: British Psychological Society, St Andrews House, 48 Princess Road East, Leicester, LE1 7DR. £650.00

Training pack comprising 4 videos, a tutor's manual, a self-help guide and a set of student support materials. Modules: 1: Presenting yourself, 2: Experts and procedures, 3: Preparing your evidence, 4: Coping with questions.

General Health

Health Action Pack: Health Education for 16–19 year olds.
Publisher: Health Education Authority, 1994.
Available from: Health Education Authority, Hamilton House, Mabledon Place, London, WC1 9TX. £55.00.

Pack containing activities for use with groups of young people which aims to identify health needs and suggest methods which might be appropriate for those needs. The pack includes background papers around the teaching of health education and includes factual information on a variety of issues. Activities include using photographs, physical activities, word games and role play.

 Love Life and Live It!
Paulene Warnock et al., 1994.
Available from: Merseyside Youth Association, 88 Sheil Road, Liverpool, L6 3AS. £12.50.

Pack provides an easily accessible programme of health education for those working with young people. There are five booklets, each giving information, activity ideas and personal experiences, together with contacts and further reading on a particular aspect of health. The five subjects covered are general health, sexuality and relationships, sexual health, HIV and drugs.

Every Woman's Health.
Health Education Authority, 1995.
Available from: WEA Publications Department, 9 Upper Berkeley Street,
London, W1H 8BY. £24.20.

A loose-leaf pack focusing on how to teach or lead sessions on health topics with
women's groups. It uses a wide variety of approaches and is equally valuable for
newcomers or experienced workers. Topics include: knowing our bodies,
motherhood, food, self and body image, emotional and mental health, relaxation
and massage, sexuality; assertiveness. Each section contains information,
activity and discussion sheets, related worksheets and notes on resources and
organisations.

 Teenagers Under Stress.
John Coleman, 1993.
Available from: TSA Publishing Ltd., 23 New Road, Brighton, East Sussex, BN1
1WZ. £8.95.

This pack is aimed at parents and all who work with young people. The pack
consists of a booklet and an audio cassette tape. Topics include: stress and its
effects, alcohol and drugs, leaving home, anti-social behaviour, problems at
school, depression, anorexia, unemployment, delinquency, pregnancy and
sexuality.

HIV/AIDS

***A Trainer's Guide to Workshops on Young People and Sexuality in the Context
of HIV/AIDS.***
Jo Burns and Cathie Wright, 1994.
Publisher: HMSO, PO Box 276, London, SW8 5DT. £11.95.

Guide designed to support trainers in running a course of four workshops for
workers working with young people around sexuality in the context of HIV/
AIDS. The workshops cover sexuality and identity, sexuality and safer sex, and
sexuality and counselling. The guide also includes recommended reading for
trainers and workers, and a number of handouts on relevant topics.

Your Choice or Mine? Personal Relationships, HIV and AIDS.
British Red Cross, 1991.
Available from: Folens Publishers, Albert House, Apex Business Centre,
Boscombe Road, Dunstable, LU5 4RL. £49.95.

A resource aimed at young people covering issues such as sexuality,
discrimination and fear. The package consists of a video containing over 50
'triggers' for discussion, trainers notes and a photocopiable fact file.

Training Aids Handbook: How to Choose, Use and Develop HIV Training Resources.
Wendy Clark, Health Education Authority, 1993.
Available from: Health Education Authority, Hamilton House, Mabledon Place, London, WC1 9TX. £6.95.

Comprehensive guide for trainers on how to choose appropriate training resources on HIV and AIDS. It looks at assessing existing training materials, developing additional resources, and exploring the issues around HIV and AIDS training. It also includes practical checklists to assist trainers in evaluating materials.

HIV/AIDS Trainers' Resource.
Chris Carne, Martin Jones and Andrew Powell, 1993.
Available from: Daniels Publishing, 38 Cambridge Place, Cambridge, CB2 1NS. £32.00.

Collection of resources intended to act as a factual base on HIV and AIDS for trainers to use with groups. It includes training materials and exercises which aim to promote the exploration of attitudes and behaviours, in order to improve understanding of HIV and AIDS issues. Sections cover definitions of HIV and AIDS, clinical features, treatment, prevention, social and psychological aspects, and helping agencies.

Our People Black HIV/AIDS Network.
Available in English, Swahili, Cantonese, Hindi, Urdu, Punjabi, Bengali and Gujarati, 1991.
Available from: Picture Talk Films, 61 Cromwell Avenue, London, N6 5HP. £86.25.

The first video aimed at Black and minority ethnic communities on the subject of HIV/AIDS. The video combines animation, interviews and true stories to explore the experiences and issues facing Black communities.

Learning Difficulties

Not Behind the Bikesheds: Health and Personal Education Students with Learning Difficulties.
Gill Combes et al., 1992.
Available from: Thomas Nelson. Nelson House, Mayfield Road, Walton on Thames, Surrey, KT12 5PL. £42.00

Teaching pack around the issues of health and personal education, designed to meet the needs of students with moderate learning difficulties. The pack consists of six units which cover a variety of issues such as self-image and assertiveness, body matters, health education, relationship, and sex and sexuality.

Improving Practice with People with Learning Disabilities: A Training Manual.
Aktar Bano et al., 1993.
Available from: CCETSW, Derbyshire House, St Chad's Street, London, WC1H 8AD. £15.00.

Training manual which focuses on education and training for anti-racist social work practice in work with Black people who have learning disabilities. Sections look at the normalisation theory and its implications for Black consumers of social services; the inter-action of race, gender, sexuality and disability; power relationships and forms of power and their implications for Black people; and the connection between race and under-achievement in mainstream and special schools.

One-To-One HIV, AIDS and You.
Department of Public Health Medicine, Stirling, 1989.
Available from: Department of Public Health Medicine, Forth Valley Health Board, 33 Spittal Street, Stirling, FK8 1DX. £25.00.

A pack for use with young people with learning disabilities, includes a 15 minute video with tutor guide designed to prompt discussion.

Leaving Home/Accommodation/Care

Working with Young People Leaving Care.
Nick Frost and Mike Stein, 1994.
Available from: HMSO Publications Centre, PO Box 276, London, SW8 5DT. £30.00.

The aim of the pack is to provide useful and accessible material which will be of practical assistance to professionals and foster carers working with young people who are being prepared for leaving, or who have left, the care of local authorities and other organisations. Designed to be as flexible as possible, it can be used as a basis for training programmes of variable length, or as a resource pack for information that is required in working with young people leaving care. Some of the materials are best used with those who are direct carers (foster carers and residential staff) and social services staff (social workers, leaving care workers and their managers). Other modules are designed to be used with inter-agency or multi-disciplinary groups.

Home Start.
Wandsworth Housing Support Project, 1992.
Available from: Wandsworth Housing Support Project, 307 Battersea Park Road, London, SW11 4LU. £5.00.

Developed for use with young people individually or in groups, this pack offers useful information to assist young people in leaving home and finding their own accommodation. The pack is made up of a number of worksheets designed to stimulate discussion, and cover issues such as benefits, gas and electricity, budgeting, health issues and emergency procedure.

✧ *Stepping Out.*
National Foster Care Association, 1991.
Available from: National Foster Care Association, Francis House, Francis Street, London, SW1P 1DE. £4.95.

Practical guide for young people in or leaving care. Provides information on housing, health, money, personal matters and the law. Also presents details on setting up home and what to look out for when moving into a new flat.

Looking After Children

It's Your Meeting: A guide to help young people get the most from their reviews.
Ann Wheal and Ruth Sinclair, 1995.
Available from: National Children's Bureau, 8 Wakley Street, London, EC1V 7QE. Single pack – £13.00, Pack of 10 – £120.00

This pack has been designed for young people aged 10 and upwards. It contains information about plans and reviews, quizzes and work searches, suggestions on preparing for reviews, how to handle meetings, sample practice reviews and a reminder telling young people about their rights at a review. The guide can be used by young people on their own, in a group or with help from older young people or carers. The pack will be invaluable to those young people who are the responsibility of social workers, residential workers, foster carers and service managers.

Looking After Children: Assessment and Action Records (Revised Version).
The Looking After Children Research and Development Team, Dartington Social Research Unit, 1995.
Available from: HMSO, PO Box 276, London, SW8 5DT.
10–14 years – £20.00 for pack of 25
15+ years – £20.00 for pack of 25.

Six age-related Assessment and Action Records are designed to promote good quality care for the children and young people 'looked after'. They are aimed to encourage communication between all those involved in the care of the young person. They should be used to assess the young person's progress in relation to the care they receive and to plan improvements. When completed at regular intervals they provide information about outcomes.

Looking After Children: Planning and Review Forms (Revised Version).
Essential Information Record Parts I and 2 – £15.00 for a pack of 25.
Care Plan – £6.00 for a pack of 25.
Placement Plan – £15.00.
The Review Form – £6.00.
The Looking After Children Research and Development Team, Dartington
Social Research Unit, 1995.
Available from: HMSO, PO Box 276, London, SW8 5DT.

Essential Information Record provides information needed by carers looking
after children in unplanned placement.
The Care Plan ensures that all children and young people looked after have
clearly stated objectives set out for their care and a strategy for achieving them.
The Placement Plan is designed to determine how best to meet day-to-day needs
during placement.
The Review Form guides the practitioner through the review process and
provides a framework for ensuring that agreed day-to-day arrangements continue
to meet the young person's needs, that overall care plan is appropriate, and the
required work still being undertaken. It is accompanied by *Consultation Papers*,
designed to help young people, parents and carers make their views known at the
review meeting.

The Looking After Children Management and Implementation Guide.
Hilary Corrick, Debbie Jones and Harriet Ward, 1995.
Available from: HMSO, PO Box 276, London, SW8 5DT. £16.99

A guide to help managers, planners and social work supervisors set up the
Looking After Children system. It includes information for those who need to
extract and analyse data from the completed forms.

The Looking After Children Training Resources Pack.
Sonia Jackson, University of Swansea and Sue Kilroe, University of Bristol,
1995.
Available from: HMSO, PO Box 276, London, SW8 5DT. £55.00

This pack contains a training guide, video, reader, practice examples and a copy
of the management and implementation guide. Training is aimed at social
workers, residential staff and foster carers. Recommended that training should be
offered either as an intensive two-day course or integrated into the
implementation process and undertaken over a 14 week period when
practitioners are beginning to use the materials in their everyday work.

Maintaining Contact

Maintaining Contact.
Barnardos, 1991.
Available from: Barnardos, Paycocke Road, Basilson, Essex, SS14 3DR.
£258.75.

A training pack on contact that was written, piloted and produced collaboratively by FRG, BAAF, NFCA, Barnardos and Jane Rowe. Provides a two-day comprehensive programme for 16 participants. The pack includes background papers, exercises, a board game, a video, notes on the Children Act 1989, and a trainer's guide. Designed for social work managers, social workers, foster carers and all who are involved in caring and planning for children.

Offending

The Nature of Adolescence: Working with Young People in Custody.
Juliet Lyon and John Coleman, 1994.
Available from: TSA Publishing, 23 New Road, Brighton, East Sussex, BN1 1WZ. £94.00.

A modular training pack which provides specialist training for staff who work with young male offenders and all those working with troubled and troublesome teenagers. Commissioned by the Prison Service, it was created by staff from the Trust for the Study of Adolescence together with men and women at all levels in the Prison Service. The pack has been shown to increase understanding and awareness among staff of young offenders' needs, feelings, problems and behaviour and to lead to a more considered approach and an improvement in staff/young person relations. The pack comprises 6 modules: introduction, adolescent development, the adolescent in the family, the peer group, offending behaviour and youth crime and the staff.

Partnership with Young People and Families

Children Act 1989: Working in Partnership with Families.
Family Rights Group, 1991.
Available from: HMSO, PO Box 276, London SW8 5DT.
Trainer's Pack – £55.00
Participants' Pack – £39.00.

A five-day training programme for 24 participants that aims to empower practitioners to empower their clients. For those who want to work in more effective partnership with families under Parts III, IV and V of the Children Act 1989. Methods are mostly small group and experiential, using case studies and other exercises. Participant's pack contains a reader file of 30 chapters and legal notes file which includes the participant's programme guide. The trainer's pack also contains a trainer's guide file.

Race

Improving Mental Health Practice: A Training Manual.
Pam Clarke, et al., 1992.
Available from: CCETSW, Derbyshire House, St Chad's Street, London,
WC1H 8AD. £18.00.

Manual written as part of a CCETSW Curriculum Development Project on anti-racist social work education, which focuses on education and training in anti-racist social work for mental health practice. Part one contains articles and extracts which focus specifically on the mental health system and its relationship with Black users. Part two consists of training materials and exercises on policy and service development, understanding the experiences of Black users, recognition of racist and sexist policy and practice, and skilled anti-racist mental health social work practice.

All Equal Under the Act? A practical guide to the Children Act for Social Workers.
Racial Equality Unit, 1991.
Available from: NISW, Mary Ward House, 5-7 Tavistock Place, London,
WC1H 9SS. £8.00.

This training pack is aimed at social workers and tackles practice problems in dealing with equal opportunities. It is made up of several sections including: social work and the history of discrimination, social work agencies and the community, the family, and children 'looked after'.

Sexuality

A Different Story: The Lives and Experiences of a Group of Young Lesbians and Gay Men.
ILEA, Video, 1987.
Available from: Educational Media International, 235 Imperial Drive, Rayners Lane, Harrow, Middlesex, HA2 7HE, (Tel: 0181-868-1908). £29.50. Running time: 50 minutes.

Two programmes for schools about a group of young people (Black and white) who have identified themselves as gay or lesbian. The first programme introduces the young people and considers the reality and strengths of the identification as gay, feelings of isolation experienced in early adolescence, experience of prejudice and the fear this creates, and responses from families, schools and friends. The second programme focuses particularly on four young people, showing them with some heterosexual friends. It looks at 'coming out' to heterosexual friends, these friends' reactions, and responses of heterosexuals in general. Teacher's notes offer guidance on the use of the video in the context of provisions of the Education Act 1988 and Department of Education and Science guidance regarding sex education.

Teenagers and Sexuality.
John Coleman with Judy Heath and Deborah Clow, 1989.
Available from: TSA Publishing Ltd., 23 New Road, Brighton, East Sussex,
BN1 1WZ. £8.95.

This pack is aimed at parents and all who work with young people. The pack consists of a booklet and an audio cassette tape. Topics include: the parents' role, sex education, sexual identity, first relationships, physical changes, contraception and AIDS.

Suicide and Self Harm

Teenage Suicide and Self Harm.
John Coleman and Juliet Lyon, 1995.
Available from: TSA Publishing Ltd., 23 New Road, Brighton, East Sussex,
BN1 1WZ. £8.95.

This pack is aimed at parents and all who work with young people. The pack consists of a booklet and an audio cassette tape. The tape consists of extracts from in-depth interviews conducted with young people who have harmed themselves or attempted suicide and interviews with their families, friends and carers. The accompanying booklet explores factors which can lead to, and behaviours associated with, deliberate self-harm or attempted suicide.

Unemployment

The Groupwork Pack: A Groupwork Approach to Problem-solving and Change.
Tim Kemp and Alan Taylor, 1990.
Available from: Longman Group Ltd., Longman House, Burnt Mill Lane,
Harlow, Essex, CM20 2JE. £19.95.

This groupwork pack has evolved from work done by the Apex Trust with disadvantaged unemployed people who not only face problems in obtaining employment, but also in other areas of their lives. The manual aims to enable people to make the most effective use of small groups in the process of problem-solving and change. Useful to trainers, teachers, social workers and counsellors, the pack contains a number of activities which cover areas of pre-group work, introductions, problem-solving and closing groups. There are also extensive notes for leaders.

Working with Young People

Working with the Children Act 1989: An Introduction for Practitioners in Education, Health and Social Work.
National Children's Bureau, 1990.
Available from: National Children's Bureau Enterprises Ltd., 8 Wakley Street, London, EC1V 7QE. £55.00 for 10 copies.

An invaluable general introduction to the principles of the Children Act, produced in easy-to-use card format. Designed for work with groups, also suitable for individual learning. Relevant to all professions dealing with children.

Teenagers in the Family.
John Coleman and Juliet Lyon, 1993.
Available from: TSA Publishing Ltd., 23 New Road, Brighton, East Sussex, BN1 1WZ. £8.95.

This pack is aimed at parents and all who work with young people. The pack looks at general issues affecting all families with teenagers. The pack consists of a booklet and an audio cassette tape. Topics include: the needs of teenagers, the needs of parents, communication and decision making, rules and regulations, conflict, the generation gap.

Residential Care and the Children Act 1989: A Resource Pack for Staff in Residential Child Care Settings.
Ruth Sinclair, 1991.
Available from: National Children's Bureau, 8 Wakley Street, London, EC1V 7QE. £4.50.

This pack, commissioned by the Department of Health, introduces staff in residential child care settings to the Children Act 1989, together with the Guidance and Regulations on Residential Care. It contains seven cards on different topics which set out what the Act says and the implications for practice. An eighth card suggests some training exercises and further resource materials.

Caring for Children and Young People.
Open University, 1985 revised 1992.
Available from: Open University, Learning Materials Sales Office, P.O. Box 188, Milton Keynes, MK7 6DH. Study pack only – £53.93, Assessment pack only – £17.00, Both packs – £70.00.

This pack is designed for people whose job involves working directly with other people's children, whether they are employed in the education, health or personal social services and whether they work for statutory organisations or voluntary organisations. The aim of the course is (a) to help inexperienced practitioners and those who have little opportunity for training to gain greater knowledge and skills around areas that their work demands; (b) to help those with little or no child care training or academic experience to develop a critical and informed approach to their work and studies; (c) to help them understand the importance to children and young people of their natural families, and how both children and families are affected when they are separated from one another.

Further information on training materials can be gained by contacting:

National Youth Agency,
17–23 Albion Street,
Leicester,
LE1 6GD.

National Children's Bureau, Enterprises Ltd.,
8 Wakley Street,
London,
EC1V 7QE.

Family Rights Group,
The Print Room,
18 Ashwin Street,
London,
E8 3DL.

Printed in the United Kingdom for HMSO
Dd302178 5/96 C30 G3397 10170

Appendix

The Advisory Group

Carolyn Davies	Principal Research Officer, Department of Health
Norman Duncan	Department of Health
Valerie Brasse	Department of Health
Ted Hillier	Department of Health
Wendy Rose	Assistant Chief Inspector, Department of Health
John Rowlands	Social Services Inspector, Department of Health
Chris Sealey	Social Services Inspector, Department of Health
Ruth Sinclair	Director of Research, National Children's Bureau
Mike Stein	Professor of Social Work, Department of Social Work and Social Policy, University of York
John Triseliotis	Emeritus Professor, International Social Sciences Institute, University of Edinburgh